KETO COOKBOOK 2022

MANY DELICIOUS RECIPES TO SURPRISE YOUR FAMILY AND FRIENDS

HANNA WILDE

Table of Contents

Simple Halloumi Salad	8
Lunch Stew	10
Chicken And Shrimp	12
Green Soup	14
Caprese Salad	16
Salmon Soup	17
Amazing Halibut Soup	19
Simple Kimchi	21
Delicious Green Beans Side Dish	23
Simple Cauliflower Mash	25
Delicious Portobello Mushrooms	27
Brussels Sprouts Side Dish	29
Delicious Pesto	31
Brussels Sprouts And Bacon	33
Delicious Spinach Side Dish	35
Amazing Avocado Fries	37
Simple Roasted Cauliflower	39
Mushroom And Spinach Side Dish	41
Delicious Okra And Tomatoes	43
Amazing Snap Peas And Mint	45
Collard Greens Side Dish	47
Eggplant And Tomato Side Dish	49
Broccoli With Lemon Almond Butter	51
Mixed Veggie Dish	53
Amazing Cauliflower Polenta	55
Amazing Side Dish	57
Special Mushrooms	61
Green Beans And Tasty Vinaigrette	63
Braised Eggplant Side Dish	65
Cheddar Soufflés	67
Tasty Cauliflower Side Salad	69
Amazing Rice	71
Delicious Marinated Eggs	73
Sausage And Cheese Dip	75
Tasty Onion And Cauliflower Dip	77

Delicious Pesto Crackers 79
Pumpkin Muffins 81
Special Tortilla Chips 83
Amazing Jalapeno Balls 85
Cheeseburger Muffins 87
Tasty Pizza Dip 89
Incredible Keto Muffins Snack 91
Amazing Fried Queso Snack 93
Maple And Pecan Bars 95
Amazing Chia Seeds Snack 97
Simple Tomato Tarts 99
Avocado Dip 101
Special Prosciutto And Shrimp Appetizer 103
Broccoli And Cheddar Biscuits 105
Tasty Corndogs 107
Tasty Pepper Nachos 109
Caprese Salad 112
Salmon Soup 113
Amazing Halibut Soup 115
Simple Kimchi 117
Delicious Green Beans Side Dish 119
Simple Cauliflower Mash 120
Delicious Portobello Mushrooms 121
Brussels Sprouts Side Dish 122
Delicious Pesto 124
Brussels Sprouts And Bacon 125
Delicious Spinach Side Dish 127
Amazing Avocado Fries 128
Simple Roasted Cauliflower 130
Mushroom And Spinach Side Dish 132
Delicious Okra And Tomatoes 134
Amazing Snap Peas And Mint 136
Collard Greens Side Dish 137
Eggplant And Tomato Side Dish 139
Broccoli With Lemon Almond Butter 140
Simple Sautéed Broccoli 142

Easy Grilled Onions	143
Sautéed Zucchinis	144
Delicious Fried Swiss Chard	146
Delicious Side Mushroom Salad	147
Greek Side Salad	149
Delicious Veal Stew	151
Veal And Tomatoes Dish	153
Veal Parmesan	154
Veal Piccata	156
Delicious Roasted Sausage	157
Baked Sausage And Kale	158
Sausage With Tomatoes And Cheese	159
Delicious Sausage Salad	161
Delicious Sausage And Peppers Soup	162
Italian Sausage Soup	164
Amazing Broccoli And Cauliflower Cream	165
Broccoli Stew	166
Amazing Watercress Soup	168
Delicious Bok Choy Soup	169
Bok Choy Stir Fry	170
Cream Of Celery	171
Delightful Celery Soup	172
Amazing Celery Stew	173
Spinach Soup	174
Delicious Mustard Greens Sauté	175
Tasty Collards Greens And Ham	176
Simple Mustard Greens Dish	178
Collard Greens Soup	181
Spring Green Soup	183
Mustard Greens And Spinach Soup	184
Roasted Asparagus	186
Simple Asparagus Fries	187
Amazing Asparagus And Browned Butter	188
Delicious Doughnuts	190
Chocolate Bombs	191
Amazing Jello Dessert	192

Strawberry Pie 193
Delicious Chocolate Pie 195
Tasty Cheesecakes 197
Raspberry And Coconut Dessert 199
Tasty Chocolate Cups 200
Simple And Delicious Mousse 201
Simple Peanut Butter Fudge 202
Lemon Mousse 203
Vanilla Ice Cream 204
Cheesecake Squares 205
Tasty Brownies 206
Chocolate Pudding 207
Vanilla Parfaits 208
Simple Avocado Pudding 209
Mint Delight 210
Amazing Coconut Pudding 211
Special Pudding 212
Chocolate Biscotti 213
Special Dessert 214
Tasty Scones 216

Simple Halloumi Salad

Just gather all the ingredients you need and enjoy one of the best keto lunches!

Preparation time: 10 minutes
Cooking time: 10 minutes
Servings: 1

Ingredients:

- 3 ounces halloumi cheese, sliced
- 1 cucumber, sliced
- 1 ounce walnuts, chopped
- A drizzle of olive oil
- A handful baby arugula
- 5 cherry tomatoes, halved
- A splash of balsamic vinegar
- Salt and black pepper to the taste

Directions:
1. Heat up your kitchen grill over medium high heat, add halloumi pieces, grill them for 5 minutes on each side and transfer to a plate.
2. In a bowl, mix tomatoes with cucumber, walnuts and arugula.
3. Add halloumi pieces on top, season everything with salt, pepper, drizzle the oil and the vinegar, toss to coat and serve.

Enjoy!

Nutrition: calories 450, fat 43, fiber 5, carbs 4, protein 21

Lunch Stew

It's so hearty and delicious! Trust us!

Preparation time: 10 minutes

Cooking time: 3 hours and 30 minutes

Servings: 6

Ingredients:

- 8 tomatoes, chopped
- 5 pounds beef shanks
- 3 carrots, chopped
- 8 garlic cloves, minced
- 2 onions, chopped
- 2 cups water
- 1-quart chicken stock
- ¼ cup tomato sauce
- Salt and black pepper to the taste
- 2 tablespoons apple cider vinegar
- 3 bay leaves
- 3 teaspoons red pepper, crushed
- 2 teaspoons parsley, dried
- 2 teaspoons basil, dried

- 2 teaspoons garlic powder
- 2 teaspoons onion powder
- A pinch of cayenne pepper

Directions:
1. Heat up a pot over medium heat, add garlic, carrots and onions, stir and brown for a few minutes.
2. Heat up a pan over medium heat, add beef shank, brown for a few minutes on each side and take off heat.
3. Add stock over carrots, the water and the vinegar and stir.
4. Add tomatoes, tomato sauce, salt, pepper, cayenne pepper, crushed pepper, bay leaves, basil, parsley, onion powder and garlic powder and stir everything.
5. Add beef shanks, cover pot, bring to a simmer and cook for 3 hours.
6. Discard bay leaves, divide into bowls and serve.

Enjoy!

Nutrition: calories 500, fat 22, fiber 4, carbs 6, protein 56

Chicken And Shrimp

It's a great combination! You'll see!

Preparation time: 10 minutes
Cooking time: 20 minutes
Servings: 2

Ingredients:

- 20 shrimp, raw, peeled and deveined
- 2 chicken breasts, boneless and skinless
- 2 handfuls spinach leaves
- ½ pound mushrooms, roughly chopped
- Salt and black pepper to the taste
- ¼ cup mayonnaise
- 2 tablespoons sriracha
- 2 teaspoons lime juice
- 1 tablespoon coconut oil
- ½ teaspoon red pepper, crushed
- 1 teaspoon garlic powder
- ½ teaspoon paprika
- ¼ teaspoon xanthan gum
- 1 green onion stalk, chopped

Directions:
1. Heat up a pan with the oil over medium high heat, add chicken breasts, season with salt, pepper, red pepper and garlic powder, cook for 8 minutes, flip and cook for 6 minutes more.
2. Add mushrooms, more salt and pepper and cook for a few minutes.
3. Heat up another pan over medium heat, add shrimp, sriracha, paprika, xanthan and mayo, stir and cook until shrimp turn pink.
4. Take off heat, add lime juice and stir everything.
5. Divide spinach on plates, divide chicken and mushroom, top with shrimp mix, garnish with green onions and serve.

Enjoy!

Nutrition: calories 500, fat 34, fiber 10, carbs 3, protein 40

Green Soup

This is just awesome!

Preparation time: 10 minutes
Cooking time: 13 minutes
Servings: 6

Ingredients:

- 1 cauliflower head, florets separated
- 1 white onion, finely chopped
- 1 bay leaf, crushed
- 2 garlic cloves, minced
- 5 ounces watercress
- 7 ounces spinach leaves
- 1-quart veggie stock
- 1 cup coconut milk
- Salt and black pepper to the taste
- ¼ cup ghee
- A handful parsley, for serving

Directions:
1. Heat up a pot with the ghee over medium high heat, add garlic and onion, stir and brown for 4 minutes.
2. Add cauliflower and bay leaf, stir and cook for 5 minutes.
3. Add watercress and spinach, stir and cook for 3 minutes.
4. Add stock, salt and pepper, stir and bring to a boil.
5. Add coconut milk, stir, take off heat and blend using an immersion blender.
6. Divide into bowls and serve right away.

Enjoy!

Nutrition: calories 230, fat 34, fiber 3, carbs 5, protein 7

Caprese Salad

This is very well known worldwide but did you know that it can be served when you are on a Ketogenic diet?

Preparation time: 5 minutes
Cooking time: 0 minutes
Servings: 2

Ingredients:

- ½ pound mozzarella cheese, sliced
- 1 tomato, sliced
- Salt and black pepper to the taste
- 4 basil leaves, torn
- 1 tablespoon balsamic vinegar
- 1 tablespoon olive oil

Directions:

1. Alternate tomato and mozzarella slices on 2 plates.
2. Sprinkle salt, pepper, drizzle vinegar and olive oil.
3. Sprinkle basil leaves at the end and serve.

Enjoy!

Nutrition: calories 150, fat 12, fiber 5, carbs 6, protein 9

Salmon Soup

This is so creamy!

Preparation time: 10 minutes

Cooking time: 25 minutes

Servings: 4

Ingredients:

- 4 leeks, trimmed and sliced
- Salt and black pepper to the taste
- 2 tablespoons avocado oil
- 2 garlic cloves, minced
- 6 cups chicken stock
- 1 pound salmon, cut into small pieces
- 2 teaspoons thyme, dried
- 1 and ¾ cups coconut milk

Directions:

1. Heat up a pot with the oil over medium heat, add leeks and garlic, stir and cook for 5 minutes.
2. Add thyme, stock, salt and pepper, stir and simmer for 15 minutes.

3. Add coconut milk and salmon, stir and bring to a simmer again.
4. Divide into bowls and serve right away.

Enjoy!

Nutrition: calories 270, fat 12, fiber 3, carbs 5, protein 32

Amazing Halibut Soup

If you are following a keto diet, then you should try this lunch idea for sure!

Preparation time: 10 minutes
Cooking time: 30 minutes
Servings: 4

Ingredients:

- 1 yellow onion, chopped
- 1 pound carrots, sliced
- 1 tablespoon coconut oil
- Salt and black pepper to the taste
- 2 tablespoons ginger, minced
- 1 cup water
- 1 pound halibut, cut into medium chunks
- 12 cups chicken stock

Directions:
1. Heat up a pot with the oil over medium heat, add onion, stir and cook for 6 minutes.
2. Add ginger, carrots, water and stock, stir bring to a simmer, reduce temperature and cook for 20 minutes.
3. Blend soup using an immersion blender, season with salt and pepper and add halibut pieces.
4. Stir gently and simmer soup for 5 minutes more.
5. Divide into bowls and serve.

Enjoy!

Nutrition: calories 140, fat 6, fiber 1, carbs 4, protein 14

Simple Kimchi

Serve this with a steak!

Preparation time: 1 hour and 10 minutes
Cooking time: 0 minutes
Servings: 6

Ingredients:
- 3 tablespoons salt
- 1 pound napa cabbage, chopped
- 1 carrot, julienned
- ½ cup daikon radish
- 3 green onion stalks, chopped
- 1 tablespoon fish sauce
- 3 tablespoons chili flakes
- 3 garlic cloves, minced
- 1 tablespoon sesame oil
- ½ inch ginger, grated

Directions:
1. In a bowl, mix cabbage with the salt, massage well for 10 minutes, cover and leave aside for 1 hour.
2. In a bowl, mix chili flakes with fish sauce, garlic, sesame oil and ginger and stir very well.

3. Drain cabbage well, rinses under cold water and transfer to a bowl.
4. Add carrots, green onions, radish and chili paste and stir everything.
5. Leave in a dark and cold place for at least 2 days before serving as a side for a keto steak.

Enjoy!

Nutrition: calories 60, fat 3, fiber 2, carbs 5, protein 1

Delicious Green Beans Side Dish

You will definitely enjoy this great side dish!

Preparation time: 10 minutes
Cooking time: 10 minutes
Servings: 4

Ingredients:

- 2/3 cup parmesan, grated
- 1 egg
- 12 ounces green beans
- Salt and black pepper to the taste
- ½ teaspoon garlic powder
- ¼ teaspoon paprika

Directions:

1. In a bowl, mix parmesan with salt, pepper, garlic powder and paprika and stir.
2. In another bowl, whisk the egg with salt and pepper.
3. Dredge green beans in egg and then in parmesan mix.

4. Place green beans on a lined baking sheet, introduce in the oven at 400 degrees F for 10 minutes.
5. Serve hot as a side dish.

Enjoy!

Nutrition: calories 114, fat 5, fiber 7, carbs 3, protein 9

Simple Cauliflower Mash

This simple Ketogenic mash goes with a meat based dish!

Preparation time: 10 minutes
Cooking time: 10 minutes
Servings: 2

Ingredients:

- ¼ cup sour cream
- 1 small cauliflower head, florets separated
- Salt and black pepper to the taste
- 2 tablespoons feta cheese, crumbled
- 2 tablespoons black olives, pitted and sliced

Directions:

1. Put water in a pot, add some salt, bring to a boil over medium heat, add florets, cook for 10 minutes, take off heat and drain.

2. Return cauliflower to the pot, add salt and black pepper to the taste and the sour cream and blend suing an immersion blender.
3. Add black olives and feta cheese, stir and serve as a side dish.

Enjoy!

Nutrition: calories 100, fat 4, fiber 2, carbs 3, protein 2

Delicious Portobello Mushrooms

These are simply the best! It's a great keto side dish!

Preparation time: 10 minutes

Cooking time: 10 minutes

Servings: 4

Ingredients:

- 12 ounces Portobello mushrooms, sliced
- Salt and black pepper to the taste
- ½ teaspoon basil, dried
- 2 tablespoons olive oil
- ½ teaspoon tarragon, dried
- ½ teaspoon rosemary, dried
- ½ teaspoon thyme, dried
- 2 tablespoons balsamic vinegar

Directions:
1. In a bowl, mix oil with vinegar, salt, pepper, rosemary, tarragon, basil and thyme and whisk well.
2. Add mushroom slices, toss to coat well, place them on your preheated grill over medium high heat, cook for 5 minutes on both sides and serve as a keto side dish.

Enjoy!

Nutrition: calories 80, fat 4, fiber 4, carbs 2, protein 4

Brussels Sprouts Side Dish

This is an Asian-style side dish you must try!

Preparation time: 10 minutes

Cooking time: 10 minutes

Servings: 4

Ingredients:

- 1 pound Brussels sprouts, trimmed and halved
- Salt and black pepper to the taste
- 1 teaspoon sesame seeds
- 1 tablespoon green onions, chopped
- 1 and ½ tablespoons sukrin gold syrup
- 1 tablespoon coconut aminos
- 2 tablespoons sesame oil
- 1 tablespoon sriracha

Directions:

1. In a bowl, mix sesame oil with coconut aminos, sriracha, syrup, salt and black pepper and whisk well.
2. Heat up a pan over medium high heat, add Brussels sprouts and cook them for 5 minutes on each side.
3. Add sesame oil mix, toss to coat, sprinkle sesame seeds and green onions, stir again and serve as a side dish.

Enjoy!

Nutrition: calories 110, fat 4, fiber 4, carbs 6, protein 4

Delicious Pesto

This keto pesto can be served with a tasty chicken dish!

Preparation time: 10 minutes

Cooking time: 0 minutes

Servings: 4

Ingredients:

- ½ cup olive oil
- 2 cups basil
- 1/3 cup pine nuts
- 1/3 cup parmesan cheese, grated
- 2 garlic cloves, chopped
- Salt and black pepper to the taste

Directions:
1. Put basil in your food processor, add pine nuts and garlic and blend very well.
2. Add parmesan, salt, pepper and the oil gradually and blend again until you obtain a paste.
3. Serve with chicken!

Enjoy!

Nutrition: calories 100, fat 7, fiber 3, carbs 1, protein 5

Brussels Sprouts And Bacon

You will love Brussels sprouts from now on!

Preparation time: 10 minutes

Cooking time: 30 minutes

Servings: 4

Ingredients:

- 8 bacon strips, chopped
- 1 pound Brussels sprouts, trimmed and halved
- Salt and black pepper to the taste
- A pinch of cumin, ground
- A pinch of red pepper, crushed
- 2 tablespoons extra virgin olive oil

Directions:

1. In a bowl, mix Brussels sprouts with salt, pepper, cumin, red pepper and oil and toss to coat.
2. Spread Brussels sprouts on a lined baking sheet, introduce in the oven at 375 degrees F and bake for 30 minutes.
3. Meanwhile, heat up a pan over medium heat, add bacon pieces and cook them until they become crispy.

4. Divide baked Brussels sprouts on plates, top with bacon and serve as a side dish right away.

Enjoy!

Nutrition: calories 256, fat 20, fiber 6, carbs 5, protein 15

Delicious Spinach Side Dish

This is very creamy and tasty!

Preparation time: 10 minutes
Cooking time: 15 minutes
Servings: 2

Ingredients:

- 2 garlic cloves, minced
- 8 ounces spinach leaves
- A drizzle of olive oil
- Salt and black pepper to the taste
- 4 tablespoons sour cream
- 1 tablespoon ghee
- 2 tablespoons parmesan cheese, grated

Directions:
1. Heat up a pan with the oil over medium heat, add spinach, stir and cook until it softens.
2. Add salt, pepper, ghee, parmesan and ghee, stir and cook for 4 minutes.
3. Add sour cream, stir and cook for 5 minutes more.
4. Divide between plates and serve as a side dish.

Enjoy!

Nutrition: calories 133, fat 10, fiber 4, carbs 4, protein 2

Amazing Avocado Fries

Try them as a side dish for a delicious steak!

Preparation time: 10 minutes
Cooking time: 5 minutes
Servings: 3

Ingredients:

- 3 avocados, pitted, peeled, halved and sliced
- 1 and ½ cups sunflower oil
- 1 and ½ cups almond meal
- A pinch of cayenne pepper
- Salt and black pepper to the taste

Directions:

1. In a bowl mix almond meal with salt, pepper and cayenne and stir.
2. In a second bowl, whisk eggs with a pinch of salt and pepper.
3. Dredge avocado pieces in egg and then in almond meal mix.
4. Heat up a pan with the oil over medium high heat, add avocado fries and cook them until they are golden.

5. Transfer to paper towels, drain grease and divide between plates.
6. Serve as a side dish.

Enjoy!

Nutrition: calories 450, fat 43, fiber 4, carbs 7, protein 17

Simple Roasted Cauliflower

This is so delicious and very easy to make at home! It's a great keto side dish!

Preparation time: 10 minutes
Cooking time: 25 minutes
Servings: 6

Ingredients:
- 1 cauliflower head, florets separated
- Salt and black pepper to the taste
- 1/3 cup parmesan, grated
- 1 tablespoon parsley, chopped
- 3 tablespoons olive oil
- 2 tablespoons extra virgin olive oil

Directions:
1. In a bowl, mix oil with garlic, salt, pepper and cauliflower florets.
2. Toss to coat well, spread this on a lined baking sheet, introduce in the oven at 450 degrees F and bake for 25 minutes, stirring halfway.

3. Add parmesan and parsley, stir and cook for 5 minutes more.
4. Divide between plates and serve as a keto side dish. Enjoy!

Nutrition: calories 118, fat 2, fiber 3, carbs 1, protein 6

Mushroom And Spinach Side Dish

This is an Italian style keto side dish worth trying as soon as possible!

Preparation time: 10 minutes
Cooking time: 10 minutes
Servings: 4

Ingredients:

- 10 ounces spinach leaves, chopped
- Salt and black pepper to the taste
- 14 ounces mushrooms, chopped
- 2 garlic cloves, minced
- A handful parsley, chopped
- 1 yellow onion, chopped
- 4 tablespoons olive oil
- 2 tablespoons balsamic vinegar

Directions:
1. Heat up a pan with the oil over medium high heat, add garlic and onion, stir and cook for 4 minutes.
2. Add mushrooms, stir and cook for 3 minutes more.
3. Add spinach, stir and cook for 3 minutes.
4. Add vinegar, salt and pepper, stir and cook for 1 minute more.
5. Add parsley, stir, divide between plates and serve hot as a side dish.

Enjoy!

Nutrition: calories 200, fat 4, fiber 6, carbs 2, protein 12

Delicious Okra And Tomatoes

This is very simple and easy to make! It's one of the best keto sides ever!

Preparation time: 10 minutes
Cooking time: 10 minutes
Servings: 6

Ingredients:

- 14 ounces canned stewed tomatoes, chopped
- Salt and black pepper to the taste
- 2 celery stalks, chopped
- 1 yellow onion, chopped
- 1 pound okra, sliced
- 2 bacon slices, chopped
- 1 small green bell peppers, chopped

Directions:

1. Heat up a pan over medium high heat, add bacon, stir, brown for a few minutes, transfer to paper towels and leave aside for now.
2. Heat up the pan again over medium heat, add okra, bell pepper, onion and celery, stir and cook for 2 minutes.

3. Add tomatoes, salt and pepper, stir and cook for 3 minutes.
4. Divide on plates, garnish with crispy bacon and serve. Enjoy!

Nutrition: calories 100, fat 2, fiber 3, carbs 2, protein 6

Amazing Snap Peas And Mint

This side dish is not just a keto one! It's a simple and quick one as well!

Preparation time: 10 minutes
Cooking time: 5 minutes
Servings: 4

Ingredients:

- ¾ pound sugar snap peas, trimmed
- Salt and black pepper to the taste
- 1 tablespoon mint leaves, chopped
- 2 teaspoons olive oil
- 3 green onions, chopped
- 1 garlic clove, minced

Directions:
1. Heat up a pan with the oil over medium high heat.
2. Add snap peas, salt, pepper, green onions, garlic and mint.
3. Stir everything, cook for 5 minutes, divide between plates and serve as a side dish for a pork steak.

Enjoy!

Nutrition: calories 70, fat 1, fiber 1, carbs 0.4, protein 6

Collard Greens Side Dish

This is just unbelievably amazing!

Preparation time: 10 minutes

Cooking time: 2 hours and 15 minutes

Servings: 10

Ingredients:

- 5 bunches collard greens, chopped
- Salt and black pepper to the taste
- 1 tablespoon red pepper flakes, crushed
- 5 cups chicken stock
- 1 turkey leg
- 2 tablespoons garlic, minced
- ¼ cup olive oil

Directions:

1. Heat up a pot with the oil over medium heat, add garlic, stir and cook for 1 minute.
2. Add stock, salt, pepper and turkey leg, stir, cover and simmer for 30 minutes.
3. Add collard greens, cover pot again and cook for 45 minutes more.

4. Reduce heat to medium, add more salt and pepper, stir and cook for 1 hour.
5. Drain greens, mix them with red pepper flakes, stir, divide between plates and serve as a side dish.

Enjoy!

Nutrition: calories 143, fat 3, fiber 4, carbs 3, protein 6

Eggplant And Tomato Side Dish

It's a keto side dish you will make over and over again!

Preparation time: 10 minutes

Cooking time: 15 minutes

Servings: 4

Ingredients:

- 1 tomato, sliced
- 1 eggplant, sliced into thin rounds
- Salt and black pepper to the taste
- ¼ cup parmesan, grated
- A drizzle of olive oil

Directions:
1. Place eggplant slices on a lined baking dish, drizzle some oil and sprinkle half of the parmesan.
2. Top eggplant slices with tomato ones, season with salt and pepper to the taste and sprinkle the rest of the cheese over them.
3. Introduce in the oven at 400 degrees F and bake for 15 minutes.
4. Divide between plates and serve hot as a side dish.

Enjoy!

Nutrition: calories 55, fat 1, fiber 1, carbs 0.5, protein 7

Broccoli With Lemon Almond Butter

This side dish is perfect for a grilled steak!

Preparation time: 10 minutes

Cooking time: 10 minutes

Servings: 4

Ingredients:

- 1 broccoli head, florets separated
- Salt and black pepper to the taste
- ¼ cup almonds, blanched
- 1 teaspoon lemon zest
- ¼ cup coconut butter, melted
- 2 tablespoons lemon juice

Directions:

1. Put water in a pot, add salt and bring to a boil over medium high heat.
2. Place broccoli florets in a steamer basket, place into the pot, cover and steam for 8 minutes.
3. Drain and transfer to a bowl.

4. Heat up a pan with the coconut butter over medium heat, add lemon juice, lemon zest and almonds, stir and take off heat.
5. Add broccoli, toss to coat, divide between plates and serve as a Ketogenic side dish.

Enjoy!

Nutrition: calories 170, fat 15, fiber 4, carbs 4, protein 4

Mixed Veggie Dish

Serve with a tasty keto steak!

Preparation time: 10 minutes
Cooking time: 10 minutes
Servings: 4

Ingredients:

- 14 ounces mushrooms, sliced
- 3 ounces broccoli florets
- 3.5 ounces sugar snap peas
- 6 tablespoons olive oil
- Salt and black pepper to the taste
- 3 ounces bell pepper, cut into strips
- 3 ounces spinach, torn
- 2 tablespoons garlic, minced
- 2 tablespoons pumpkin seeds
- A pinch of red pepper flakes

Directions:
1. Heat up a pan with the oil over medium high heat, add garlic, stir and cook for 1 minute.
2. Add mushrooms, stir and cook for 3 minutes more.
3. Add broccoli and stir everything.
4. Add snap peas and peppers and stir again.
5. Add salt, pepper, pumpkin seeds and pepper flakes, stir and cook for a few minutes.
6. Add spinach, stir gently, cook for a couple of minutes, divide between plates and serve as a side dish.

Enjoy!

Nutrition: calories 247, fat 23, fiber 4, carbs 3, protein 7

Amazing Cauliflower Polenta

This should be very interesting! Let's learn how to prepare it!

Preparation time: 10 minutes

Cooking time: 1 hour

Servings: 2

Ingredients:

- 1 cauliflower head, florets separated and chopped
- ¼ cup hazelnuts
- 1 tablespoon olive oil + 2 teaspoons extra virgin olive oil
- 1 small yellow onion, chopped
- 3 cups shiitake mushrooms, chopped
- 4 garlic cloves
- 3 tablespoons nutritional yeast
- ½ cup water
- Chopped parsley for serving

Directions:

1. Spread hazelnuts on a lined baking sheet, introduce in the oven at 350 degrees F and bake for 10 minutes.

2. Take hazelnuts out of the oven, leave them to cool down, chop and leave aside for now.
3. Spread cauliflower florets on the baking sheet, drizzle 1 teaspoon oil, introduce in the oven at 400 degrees F and bake for 30 minutes.
4. In a bowl, mix oil with ½ teaspoon oil and toss to coat.
5. Put garlic cloves on a tin foil, drizzle ½ teaspoon oil and wrap.
6. Spread onion next to cauliflower, also add wrapped garlic to the baking sheet, introduce in the oven everything and bake for 20 minutes.
7. Heat up a pan with the rest of the oil over medium high heat, add mushrooms, stir and cook for 8 minutes.
8. Take cauliflower out of the oven and transfer to your food processor.
9. Unwrap garlic, peel and also add to the food processor.
10. Add onion, yeast, salt and pepper and blend everything well.
11. Divide polenta on plates, top with mushrooms, hazelnuts and parsley and serve as a side.

Enjoy!

Nutrition: calories 342, fat 21, fiber 12, carbs 3, protein 14

Amazing Side Dish

This will totally surprise you!

Preparation time: 10 minutes
Cooking time: 4 hours and 20 minutes
Servings: 8

Ingredients:
- 2 cups almond flour
- 2 tablespoons whey protein powder
- ¼ cup coconut flour
- ½ teaspoon garlic powder
- 2 teaspoons baking powder
- 1 and ¼ cups cheddar cheese, shredded
- 2 eggs
- ¼ cup melted ghee
- ¾ cup water

For the stuffing:
- ½ cup yellow onion, chopped
- 2 tablespoons ghee
- 1 red bell pepper, chopped
- 1 jalapeno pepper, chopped

- Salt and black pepper to the taste
- 12 ounces sausage, chopped
- 2 eggs
- ¾ cup chicken stock
- ¼ cup whipping cream

Directions:

1. In a bowl, mix coconut flour with whey protein, almond flour, garlic powder, baking powder and 1 cup cheddar cheese and stir everything.
2. Add water, 2 eggs and ¼ cup ghee and stir well.
3. Transfer this to a greased baking pan, sprinkle the rest of the cheddar cheese, introduce in the oven at 325 degrees F and bake for 30 minutes.
4. Leave the bread to cool down for 15 minutes and cube it.
5. Spread bread cubes on a lined baking sheet, introduce in the oven at 200 degrees F and bake for 3 hours.
6. Take bread cubes out of the oven and leave aside for now.
7. Heat up a pan with 2 tablespoons ghee over medium heat, add onion, stir and cook for 4 minutes.
8. Add jalapeno and red bell pepper, stir and cook for 5 minutes.
9. Add salt and pepper, stir and transfer everything to a bowl.
10. Heat up the same pan over medium heat, add sausage, stir and cook for 10 minutes.
11. Transfer to the bowl with the veggies, also add stock, bread and stir everything.

12. In a separate bowl, whisk 2 eggs with some salt, pepper and whipping cream.
13. Add this to sausage and bread mix, stir, transfer to a greased baking pan, introduce in the oven at 325 degrees F and bake for 30 minutes.
14. Serve hot as a side.

Enjoy!

Nutrition: calories 340, fat 4, fiber 6, carbs 3.4, protein 7

Special Mushrooms

It's so yummy! You have to try it to see!

Preparation time: 10 minutes

Cooking time: 30 minutes

Servings: 4

Ingredients:
- 4 tablespoons ghee
- 16 ounces baby mushrooms
- Salt and black pepper to the taste
- 3 tablespoons onion, dried
- 3 tablespoons parsley flakes
- 1 teaspoon garlic powder

Directions:
1. In a bowl, mix parsley flakes with onion, salt, pepper and garlic powder and stir.
2. In another bowl, mix mushroom with melted ghee and toss to coat.
3. Add seasoning mix, toss well, spread on a lined baking sheet, introduce in the oven at 300 degrees F and bake for 30 minutes.
4. Serve as a side dish for a tasty keto roast.

Enjoy!

Nutrition: calories 152, fat 12, fiber 5, carbs 6, protein 4

Green Beans And Tasty Vinaigrette

You will find this keto side dish really amazing!

Preparation time: 10 minutes

Cooking time: 12 minutes

Serving: 8

Ingredients:

- 2 ounces chorizo, chopped
- 1 garlic clove, minced
- 1 teaspoon lemon juice
- 2 teaspoons smoked paprika
- ½ cup coconut vinegar
- 4 tablespoons macadamia nut oil
- ¼ teaspoon coriander, ground
- Salt and black pepper to the taste
- 2 tablespoons coconut oil
- 2 tablespoons beef stock
- 2 pound green beans

Directions:

1. In a blender, mix chorizo with salt, pepper, vinegar, garlic, lemon juice, paprika and coriander and pulse well.
2. Add the stock and the macadamia nut oil and blend again.
3. Heat up a pan with the coconut oil over medium heat, add green beans and chorizo mix, stir and cook for 10 minutes.
4. Divide between plates and serve.

Enjoy!

Nutrition: calories 160, fat 12, fiber 4, carbs 6, protein 4

Braised Eggplant Side Dish

Try this Vietnamese keto side dish!

Preparation time: 10 minutes
Cooking time: 15 minutes
Servings: 4

Ingredients:

- 1 big Asian eggplant, cut into medium pieces
- 1 yellow onion, thinly sliced
- 2 tablespoon vegetable oil
- 2 teaspoons garlic, minced
- ½ cup Vietnamese sauce
- ½ cup water
- 2 teaspoons chili paste
- ¼ cup coconut milk
- 4 green onions, chopped

For the Vietnamese sauce:

- 1 teaspoon palm sugar
- ½ cup chicken stock
- 2 tablespoons fish sauce

Directions:
1. Put stock in a pan and heat up over medium heat.
2. Add sugar and fish sauce, stir well and leave aside for now.
3. Heat up a pan over medium high heat, add eggplant pieces, brown them for 2 minutes and transfer to a plate.
4. Heat up the pan again with the oil over medium high heat, add yellow onion and garlic, stir and cook for 2 minutes.
5. Return eggplant pieces and cook for 2 minutes.
6. Add water, the Vietnamese sauce you've made earlier, chili paste and coconut milk, stir and cook for 5 minutes.
7. Add green onions, stir, cook for 1 minute more, transfer to plates and serve as a side dish.

Enjoy!

Nutrition: calories 142, fat 7, fiber 4, carbs 5, protein 3

Cheddar Soufflés

If you are on a Ketogenic diet, then you must really try this side dish! Serve with a steak on the side!

Preparation time: 10 minutes
Cooking time: 25 minutes
Servings: 8

Ingredients:

- ¾ cup heavy cream
- 2 cups cheddar cheese, shredded
- 6 eggs
- Salt and black pepper to the taste
- ¼ teaspoon cream of tartar
- A pinch of cayenne pepper
- ½ teaspoon xanthan gum
- 1 teaspoon mustard powder
- ¼ cup chives, chopped
- ½ cup almond flour
- Cooking spray

Directions:

1. In a bowl, mix almond flour with salt, pepper, mustard, xanthan gum and cayenne and whisk well.
2. Add cheese, cream, chives, eggs and cream of tartar and whisk well again.
3. Grease 8 ramekins with cooking spray, pour cheddar and chives mix, introduce in the oven at 350 degrees F and bake for 25 minutes.
4. Serve your soufflés with a tasty keto steak.

Enjoy!

Nutrition: calories 288, fat 23, fiber 1, carbs 3.3, protein 14

Tasty Cauliflower Side Salad

This is much better than you could ever imagine!

Preparation time: 10 minutes

Cooking time: 5 minutes

Servings: 10

Ingredients:

- 21 ounces cauliflower, florets separated
- Salt and black pepper to the taste
- 1 cup red onion, chopped
- 1 cup celery, chopped
- 2 tablespoons cider vinegar
- 1 teaspoon splenda
- 4 eggs, hard-boiled, peeled and chopped
- 1 cup mayonnaise
- 1 tablespoon water

Directions:

1. Put cauliflower florets in a heatproof bowl, add the water, cover and cook in your microwave for 5 minutes.

2. Leave aside for another 5 minutes and transfer to a salad bowl.
3. Add celery, eggs and onions and stir gently.
4. In a bowl, mix mayo with salt, pepper, splenda and vinegar and whisk well.
5. Add this to salad, toss to coat well and serve right away with a side salad.

Enjoy!

Nutrition: calories 211, fat 20, fiber 2, carbs 3, protein 4

Amazing Rice

Don't worry! It's not made with actual rice!

Preparation time: 10 minutes
Cooking time: 30 minutes
Servings: 4

Ingredients:

- 1 cauliflower head, florets separated
- Salt and black pepper to the taste
- 10 ounces coconut milk
- ½ cup water
- 2 ginger slices
- 2 tablespoons coconut shreds, toasted

Directions:

1. Put cauliflower in your food processor and blend.
2. Transfer cauliflower rice to a kitchen towel, press well and leave aside.
3. Heat up a pot with the coconut milk over medium heat.
4. Add the water and ginger, stir and bring to a simmer.
5. Add cauliflower, stir and cook for 30 minutes.

6. Discard ginger, add salt, pepper and coconut shreds, stir gently, divide between plates and serve as a side for a poultry based dish.

Enjoy!

Nutrition: calories 108, fat 3, fiber 6, carbs 5, protein 9

Delicious Marinated Eggs

It's a fact! These are delicious!

Preparation time: 2 hours and 10 minutes
Cooking time: 7 minutes
Servings: 4

Ingredients:

- 6 eggs
- 1 and ¼ cups water
- ¼ cup unsweetened rice vinegar
- 2 tablespoons coconut aminos
- Salt and black pepper to the taste
- 2 garlic cloves, minced
- 1 teaspoon stevia
- 4 ounces cream cheese
- 1 tablespoon chives, chopped

Directions:

1. Put the eggs in a pot, add water to cover, bring to a boil over medium heat, cover and cook for 7 minutes.
2. Rinse eggs with cold water and leave them aside to cool down.

3. In a bowl, mix 1 cup water with coconut aminos, vinegar, stevia and garlic and whisk well.
4. Put the eggs in this mix, cover with a kitchen towel and leave them aside for 2 hours rotating from time to time.
5. Peel eggs, cut in halves and put egg yolks in a bowl.
6. Add ¼ cup water, cream cheese, salt, pepper and chives and stir well.
7. Stuff egg whites with this mix and serve them.

Enjoy!

Nutrition: calories 210, fat 3, fiber 1, carbs 3, protein 12

Sausage And Cheese Dip

This is a great appetizer or snack idea!

Preparation time: 10 minutes
Cooking time: 2 hours and 10 minutes
Servings: 28

Ingredients:

- 8 ounces cream cheese
- A pinch of salt and black pepper
- 16 ounces sour cream
- 8 ounces pepper jack cheese, chopped
- 15 ounces canned tomatoes mixed with habaneros
- 1 pound Italian sausage, ground
- ¼ cup green onions, chopped

Directions:

1. Heat up a pan over medium heat, add sausage, stir and cook until it browns.
2. Add tomatoes mix, stir and cook for 4 minutes more.
3. Add a pinch of salt, pepper and the green onions, stir and cook for 4 minutes.

4. Spread pepper jack cheese on the bottom of your slow cooker.
5. Add cream cheese, sausage mix and sour cream, cover and cook on High for 2 hours.
6. Uncover your slow cooker, stir dip, transfer to a bowl and serve.

Enjoy!

Nutrition: calories 144, fat 12, fiber 1, carbs 3, protein 6

Tasty Onion And Cauliflower Dip

It's a really amazing combination! Try it!

Preparation time: 2 hours 10 minutes
Cooking time: 30 minutes
Servings: 24

Ingredients:

- 1 and ½ cups chicken stock
- 1 cauliflower head, florets separated
- ¼ cup mayonnaise
- ½ cup yellow onion, chopped
- ¾ cup cream cheese
- ½ teaspoon chili powder
- ½ teaspoon cumin, ground
- ½ teaspoon garlic powder
- Salt and black pepper to the taste

Directions:

1. Put the stock in a pot, add cauliflower and onion, heat up over medium heat and cook for 30 minutes.
2. Add chili powder, salt, pepper, cumin and garlic powder and stir.

3. Also add cream cheese and stir a bit until it melts.
4. Blend using an immersion blender and mix with the mayo.
5. Transfer to a bowl and keep in the fridge for 2 hours before you serve it.

Enjoy!

Nutrition: calories 60, fat 4, fiber 1, carbs 1, protein 1

Delicious Pesto Crackers

It's one of the tastiest keto snacks ever!

Preparation time: 10 minutes
Cooking time: 17 minutes
Servings: 6

Ingredients:

- ½ teaspoon baking powder
- Salt and black pepper to the taste
- 1 and ¼ cups almond flour
- ¼ teaspoon basil, dried
- 1 garlic clove, minced
- 2 tablespoons basil pesto
- A pinch of cayenne pepper
- 3 tablespoons ghee

Directions:

1. In a bowl, mix salt, pepper, baking powder and almond flour.
2. Add garlic, cayenne and basil and stir.
3. Add pesto and whisk.
4. Also add ghee and mix your dough with your finger.

5. Spread this dough on a lined baking sheet, introduce in the oven at 325 degrees F and bake for 17 minutes.
6. Leave aside to cool down, cut your crackers and serve them as a snack.

Enjoy!

Nutrition: calories 200, fat 20, fiber 1, carbs 4, protein 7

Pumpkin Muffins

You can even take this snack at the office!

Preparation time: 10 minutes
Cooking time: 15 minutes
Servings: 18

Ingredients:

- ¼ cup sunflower seed butter
- ¾ cup pumpkin puree
- 2 tablespoons flaxseed meal
- ¼ cup coconut flour
- ½ cup erythritol
- ½ teaspoon nutmeg, ground
- 1 teaspoon cinnamon, ground
- ½ teaspoon baking soda
- 1 egg
- ½ teaspoon baking powder
- A pinch of salt

Directions:

1. In a bowl, mix butter with pumpkin puree and egg and blend well.
2. Add flaxseed meal, coconut flour, erythritol, baking soda, baking powder, nutmeg, cinnamon and a pinch of salt and stir well.
3. Spoon this into a greased muffin pan, introduce in the oven at 350 degrees F and bake for 15 minutes.
4. Leave muffins to cool down and serve them as a snack. Enjoy!

Nutrition: calories 50, fat 3, fiber 1, carbs 2, protein 2

Special Tortilla Chips

It's an exceptional keto snack recipe!

Preparation time: 10 minutes
Cooking time: 14 minutes
Servings: 6

Ingredients:

For the tortillas:
- 2 teaspoons olive oil
- 1 cup flax seed meal
- 2 tablespoons psyllium husk powder
- ¼ teaspoon xanthan gum
- 1 cup water
- ½ teaspoon curry powder
- 3 teaspoons coconut flour

For the chips:
- 6 flaxseed tortillas
- Salt and black pepper to the taste
- 3 tablespoons vegetable oil
- Fresh salsa for serving
- Sour cream for serving

Directions:
1. In a bowl, mix flaxseed meal with psyllium powder, olive oil, xanthan gum, water and curry powder and mix until you obtain an elastic dough.
2. Spread coconut flour on a working surface.
3. Divide dough into 6 pieces, place each piece on the working surface and roll into a circle and cut each into 6 pieces.
4. Heat up a pan with the vegetable oil over medium high heat, add tortilla chips, cook for 2 minutes on each side and transfer to paper towels.
5. Put tortilla chips in a bowl, season with salt and pepper and serve with some fresh salsa and sour cream on the side.

Enjoy!

Nutrition: calories 30, fat 3, fiber 1.2, carbs 0.5, protein 1

Amazing Jalapeno Balls

These are easy to make but they are so flavored and delicious!

Preparation time: 10 minutes
Cooking time: 10 minutes
Servings: 3

Ingredients:

- 3 bacon slices
- 3 ounces cream cheese
- ¼ teaspoon onion powder
- Salt and black pepper to the taste
- 1 jalapeno pepper, chopped
- ½ teaspoon parsley, dried
- ¼ teaspoon garlic powder

Directions:

1. Heat up a pan over medium high heat, add bacon, cook until it's crispy, transfer to paper towels, drain grease and crumble.
2. Reserve bacon fat from the pan.
3. In a bowl, mix cream cheese with jalapeno pepper, onion and garlic powder, parsley, salt and pepper and stir well.

4. Add bacon fat and bacon crumbles, stir gently, shape balls from this mix and serve.

Enjoy!

Nutrition: calories 200, fat 18, fiber 1, carbs 2, protein 5

Cheeseburger Muffins

This is a great keto appetizer for a sports night!

Preparation time: 10 minutes
Cooking time: 30 minutes
Servings: 9

Ingredients:
- ½ cup flaxseed meal
- ½ cup almond flour
- Salt and black pepper to the taste
- 2 eggs
- 1 teaspoon baking powder
- ¼ cups sour cream

For the filling:
- ½ teaspoon onion powder
- 16 ounces beef, ground
- Salt and black pepper to the taste
- 2 tablespoons tomato paste
- ½ teaspoon garlic powder
- ½ cup cheddar cheese, grated
- 2 tablespoons mustard

Directions:
1. In a bowl, mix almond flour with flaxseed meal, salt, pepper and baking powder and whisk.
2. Add eggs and sour cream and stir very well.
3. Divide this into a greased muffin pan and press well using your fingers.
4. Heat up a pan over medium high heat, add beef, stir and brown for a few minutes.
5. Add salt, pepper, onion powder, garlic powder and tomato paste and stir well.
6. Cook for 5 minutes more and take off heat.
7. Fill cupcakes crusts with this mix, introduce in the oven at 350 degrees F and bake for 15 minutes.
8. Spread cheese on top, introduce in the oven again and bake muffins for 5 minutes more.
9. Serve with mustard and your favorite toppings on top.

Enjoy!

Nutrition: calories 245, fat 16, fiber 6, carbs 2, protein 14

Tasty Pizza Dip

You will love this great dip!

Preparation time: 10 minutes
Cooking time: 20 minutes
Servings: 4

Ingredients:

- 4 ounces cream cheese, soft
- ½ cup mozzarella cheese
- ¼ cup sour cream
- Salt and black pepper to the taste
- 1/2 cup tomato sauce
- ¼ cup mayonnaise
- ¼ cup parmesan cheese, grated
- 1 tablespoon green bell pepper, chopped
- 6 pepperoni slices, chopped
- ½ teaspoon Italian seasoning
- 4 black olives, pitted and chopped

Directions:

1. In a bowl, mix cream cheese with mozzarella, sour cream, mayo, salt and pepper and stir well.
2. Spread this into 4 ramekins, add a layer of tomato sauce, then layer parmesan cheese, top with bell pepper, pepperoni, Italian seasoning and black olives.
3. Introduce in the oven at 350 degrees F and bake for 20 minutes.
4. Serve warm.

Enjoy!

Nutrition: calories 400, fat 34, fiber 4, carbs 4, protein 15

Incredible Keto Muffins Snack

Everyone appreciates a great treat! Try this one soon!

Preparation time: 10 minutes
Cooking time: 15 minutes
Servings: 20

Ingredients:

- ½ cup flaxseed meal
- ½ cup almond flour
- 3 tablespoons swerve
- 1 tablespoon psyllium powder
- A pinch of salt
- Cooking spray
- ¼ teaspoon baking powder
- 1 egg
- ¼ cup coconut milk
- 1/3 cup sour cream
- 3 hot dogs, cut into 20 pieces

Directions:

1. In a bowl, mix flaxseed meal with flour, psyllium powder, swerve, salt and baking powder and stir.
2. Add egg, sour cream and coconut milk and whisk well.
3. Grease a muffin tray with cooking oil, divide the batter you've just make, stick a hot dog piece in the middle of each muffin, introduce in the oven at 350 degrees F and bake for 12 minutes.
4. Broil in preheated broil for 3 minutes more, divide on a platter and serve.

Enjoy!

Nutrition: calories 80, fat 6, fiber 1, carbs 1, protein 3

Amazing Fried Queso Snack

It's a crispy and tasty keto snack!

Preparation time: 10 minutes
Cooking time: 10 minutes
Servings: 6

Ingredients:

- 2 ounces olives, pitted and chopped
- 5 ounces queso Blanco, cubed and freeze for a couple of minutes
- A pinch of red pepper flakes
- 1 and ½ tablespoons olive oil

Directions:

1. Heat up a pan with the oil over medium high heat, add queso cubes and cook until the bottom melts a bit.
2. Flip cubes with a spatula and sprinkle black olives on top.
3. Leave cubes to cook a bit more, flip and sprinkle red pepper flakes and cook until they are crispy.

4. Flip, cook on the other side until it's crispy as well, transfer to a cutting board, cut into small blocks and then serve as a snack.

Enjoy!

Nutrition: calories 500, fat 43, fiber 4, carbs 2, protein 30

Maple And Pecan Bars

This is a very healthy keto snack for you to try soon!

Preparation time: 10 minutes
Cooking time: 25 minutes
Servings: 12

Ingredients:

- ½ cup flaxseed meal
- 2 cups pecans, toasted and crushed
- 1 cup almond flour
- ½ cup coconut oil
- ¼ teaspoon stevia
- ½ cup coconut, shredded
- ¼ cup "maple syrup"

For the maple syrup:

- ¼ cup erythritol
- 2 and ¼ teaspoons coconut oil
- 1 tablespoon ghee
- ¼ teaspoon xanthan gum
- ¾ cup water
- 2 teaspoons maple extract

- ½ teaspoon vanilla extract

Directions:
1. In a heatproof bowl, mix ghee with 2 and ¼ teaspoons coconut oil and xanthan gum, stir, introduce in your microwave and heat up for 1 minute.
2. Add erythritol, water, maple and vanilla extract, stir well and heat up in the microwave for 1 minute more.
3. In a bowl, mix flaxseed meal with coconut and almond flour and stir.
4. Add pecans and stir again.
5. Add ¼ cup "maple syrup", stevia and ½ cup coconut oil and stir well.
6. Spread this in a baking dish, press well, introduce in the oven at 350 degrees F and bake for 25 minutes.
7. Leave aside to cool down, cut into 12 bars and serve as a keto snack.

Enjoy!

Nutrition: calories 300, fat 30, fiber 12, carbs 2, protein 5

Amazing Chia Seeds Snack

Try these tasty crackers today!

Preparation time: 10 minutes
Cooking time: 35 minutes
Servings: 36

Ingredients:

- 1 and ¼ cup ice water
- ½ cup chia seeds, ground
- 3 ounces cheddar, cheese, grated
- ¼ teaspoon xanthan gum
- 2 tablespoons olive oil
- 2 tablespoons psyllium husk powder
- ¼ teaspoon oregano, dried
- ¼ teaspoon garlic powder
- ¼ teaspoon onion powder
- Salt and black pepper to the taste
- ¼ teaspoon sweet paprika

Directions:

1. In a bowl, mix chia seeds with xanthan gum, psyllium powder, oregano, garlic and onion powder, paprika, salt and pepper and stir.
2. Add oil and stir well.
3. Add ice water and stir until you obtain a firm dough.
4. Spread this on a baking sheet, introduce in the oven at 350 degrees F and bake for 35 minutes.
5. Leave aside to cool down, cut into 36 crackers and serve them as a keto snack.

Enjoy!

Nutrition: calories 50, fat 3, fiber 1, carbs 0.1, protein 2

Simple Tomato Tarts

These are simple, yet very tasty keto appetizers!

Preparation time: 10 minutes
Cooking time: 1 hour and 10 minutes
Servings: 12

Ingredients:

- ¼ cup olive oil
- 2 tomatoes, sliced
- Salt and black pepper to the taste

For the base:

- 5 tablespoons ghee
- 1 tablespoon psyllium husk
- ½ cup almond flour
- 2 tablespoons coconut flour
- A pinch of salt

For the filling:

- 2 teaspoons garlic, minced
- 3 teaspoons thyme, chopped
- 2 tablespoons olive oil
- 3 ounces goat cheese, crumbled
- 1 small onion, thinly sliced

Directions:

1. Spread tomato slices on a lined baking sheet, season with salt and pepper, drizzle ¼ cup olive oil, introduce in the oven at 425 degrees F and bake for 40 minutes.
2. Meanwhile, in your food processor mix almond flour with psyllium husk, coconut flour, salt, pepper and cold butter and stir until you obtain a dough.
3. Divide this dough into silicone cupcake molds, press well, introduce in the oven at 350 degrees F and bake for 20 minutes.
4. Take cupcakes out of the oven and leave aside.
5. Also take tomato slices out of the oven and cool them down a bit.
6. Divide tomato slices on top of cupcakes.
7. Heat up a pan with 2 tablespoons olive oil over medium high heat, add onion, stir and cook for 4 minutes.
8. Add garlic and thyme, stir, cook for 1 minute more and take off heat.
9. Spread this mix on top of tomato slices.
10. Sprinkle goat cheese, introduce in the oven again and cook at 350 degrees F for 5 minutes more.
11. Arrange on a platter and serve.

Enjoy!

Nutrition: calories 163, fat 13, fiber 1, carbs 3, protein 3

Avocado Dip

This is not a guacamole but it's equally delicious!

Preparation time: 3 hours and 10 minutes
Cooking time: 10 minutes
Servings: 4

Ingredients:

- ¼ cup erythritol powder
- 2 avocados, pitted, peeled and cut into slices
- ¼ teaspoon stevia
- ½ cup cilantro, chopped
- Juice and zest of 2 limes
- 1 cup coconut milk

Directions:

1. Place avocado slices on a lined baking sheet, squeeze half of the lime juice over them and keep in your freezer for 3 hours.
2. Heat up the coconut milk in a pan over medium heat.
3. Add lime zest, stir and bring to a boil.
4. Add erythritol powder, stir, take off heat and leave aside to cool down a bit.

5. Transfer avocado to your food processor, add the rest of the lime juice and the cilantro and pulse well.
6. Add coconut milk mix and stevia and blend well.
7. Transfer to a bowl and serve right away.

Enjoy!

Nutrition: calories 150, fat 14, fiber 2, carbs 4, protein 2

Special Prosciutto And Shrimp Appetizer

You've got to love this! It's tasty!

Preparation time: 10 minutes
Cooking time: 20 minutes
Servings: 16

Ingredients:

- 2 tablespoons olive oil
- 10 ounces already cooked shrimp, peeled and deveined
- 1 tablespoons mint, chopped
- 2 tablespoons erythritol
- 1/3 cup blackberries, ground
- 11 prosciutto sliced
- 1/3 cup red wine

Directions:

1. Wrap each shrimp in prosciutto slices, arrange on a lined baking sheet, drizzle the olive oil over them, introduce in the oven at 425 degrees F and bake for 15 minutes.

2. Heat up a pan with ground blackberries over medium heat, add mint, wine and erythritol, stir, cook for 3 minutes and take off heat.
3. Arrange shrimp on a platter, drizzle blackberries sauce over them and serve.

Enjoy!

Nutrition: calories 245, fat 12, fiber 2, carbs 1, protein 14

Broccoli And Cheddar Biscuits

This snack will really make you feel full for a couple of hours!

Preparation time: 10 minutes

Cooking time: 25 minutes

Servings: 12

Ingredients:

- 4 cups broccoli florets
- 1 and ½ cup almond flour
- 1 teaspoon paprika
- Salt and black pepper to the taste
- 2 eggs
- ¼ cup coconut oil
- 2 cups cheddar cheese, grated
- 1 teaspoon garlic powder
- ½ teaspoon apple cider vinegar
- ½ teaspoon baking soda

Directions:

1. Put broccoli florets in your food processor, add some salt and pepper and blend well.

2. In a bowl, mix almond flour with salt, pepper, paprika, garlic powder and baking soda and stir.
3. Add cheddar cheese, coconut oil, eggs and vinegar and stir everything.
4. Add broccoli and stir again.
5. Shape 12 patties, arrange on a baking sheet, introduce in the oven at 375 degrees F and bake for 20 minutes.
6. Turn the oven to broiler and broil your biscuits for 5 minutes more.
7. Arrange on a platter and serve.

Enjoy!

Nutrition: calories 163, fat 12, fiber 2, carbs 2, protein 7

Tasty Corndogs

These are so delicious and simple to make!

Preparation time: 10 minutes
Cooking time: 10 minutes
Servings: 4

Ingredients:

- 1 and ½ cups olive oil
- 2 tablespoons heavy cream
- 1 cup almond meal
- 4 sausages
- 1 teaspoon baking powder
- 1 teaspoon Italian seasoning
- 2 eggs
- ½ teaspoon turmeric
- Salt and black pepper to the taste
- A pinch of cayenne pepper

Directions:

1. In a bowl, mix almond meal with Italian seasoning, baking powder, turmeric, salt, pepper and cayenne and stir well.
2. In another bowl, mix eggs with heavy cream and whisk well.
3. Combine the 2 mixtures and stir well.
4. Dip sausages in this mix and place them on a plate.
5. Heat up a pan with the oil over medium high heat, add sausages, cook for 2 minutes on each side and transfer to paper towels.
6. Drain grease, arrange on a platter and serve.

Enjoy!

Nutrition: calories 345, fat 33, fiber 4, carbs 5, protein 16

Tasty Pepper Nachos

These look wonderful! They are so tasty and healthy!

Preparation time: 10 minutes
Cooking time: 20 minutes
Servings: 6

Ingredients:

- 1 pound mini bell peppers, cut in halves
- Salt and black pepper to the taste
- 1 teaspoon garlic powder
- 1 teaspoon sweet paprika
- ½ teaspoon oregano, dried
- ¼ teaspoon red pepper flakes
- 1 pound beef meat, ground
- 1 and ½ cups cheddar cheese, shredded
- 1 tablespoons chili powder
- 1 teaspoon cumin, ground
- ½ cup tomato, chopped
- Sour cream for serving

Directions:

1. In a bowl, mix chili powder with paprika, salt, pepper, cumin, oregano, pepper flakes and garlic powder and stir.
2. Heat up a pan over medium heat, add beef, stir and brown for 10 minutes.
3. Add chili powder mix, stir and take off heat.
4. Arrange pepper halves on a lined baking sheet, stuff them with the beef mix, sprinkle cheese, introduce in the oven at 400 degrees F and bake for 10 minutes.
5. Take peppers out of the oven, sprinkle tomatoes and divide between plates and serve with sour cream on top.

Enjoy!

Nutrition: calories 350, fat 22, fiber 3, carbs 6, protein 27

Caprese Salad

This is very well known worldwide but did you know that it can be served when you are on a Ketogenic diet?

Preparation time: 5 minutes
Cooking time: 0 minutes
Servings: 2

Ingredients:

- ½ pound mozzarella cheese, sliced
- 1 tomato, sliced
- Salt and black pepper to the taste
- 4 basil leaves, torn
- 1 tablespoon balsamic vinegar
- 1 tablespoon olive oil

Directions:

4. Alternate tomato and mozzarella slices on 2 plates.
5. Sprinkle salt, pepper, drizzle vinegar and olive oil.
6. Sprinkle basil leaves at the end and serve.

Enjoy!

Nutrition: calories 150, fat 12, fiber 5, carbs 6, protein 9

Salmon Soup

This is so creamy!

Preparation time: 10 minutes
Cooking time: 25 minutes
Servings: 4

Ingredients:

- 4 leeks, trimmed and sliced
- Salt and black pepper to the taste
- 2 tablespoons avocado oil
- 2 garlic cloves, minced
- 6 cups chicken stock
- 1 pound salmon, cut into small pieces
- 2 teaspoons thyme, dried
- 1 and ¾ cups coconut milk

Directions:

5. Heat up a pot with the oil over medium heat, add leeks and garlic, stir and cook for 5 minutes.
6. Add thyme, stock, salt and pepper, stir and simmer for 15 minutes.

7. Add coconut milk and salmon, stir and bring to a simmer again.
8. Divide into bowls and serve right away.

Enjoy!

Nutrition: calories 270, fat 12, fiber 3, carbs 5, protein 32

Amazing Halibut Soup

If you are following a keto diet, then you should try this lunch idea for sure!

Preparation time: 10 minutes
Cooking time: 30 minutes
Servings: 4

Ingredients:

- 1 yellow onion, chopped
- 1 pound carrots, sliced
- 1 tablespoon coconut oil
- Salt and black pepper to the taste
- 2 tablespoons ginger, minced
- 1 cup water
- 1 pound halibut, cut into medium chunks
- 12 cups chicken stock

Directions:

6. Heat up a pot with the oil over medium heat, add onion, stir and cook for 6 minutes.
7. Add ginger, carrots, water and stock, stir bring to a simmer, reduce temperature and cook for 20 minutes.

8. Blend soup using an immersion blender, season with salt and pepper and add halibut pieces.

9. Stir gently and simmer soup for 5 minutes more.
10. Divide into bowls and serve.

Enjoy!

Nutrition: calories 140, fat 6, fiber 1, carbs 4, protein 14

Simple Kimchi

Serve this with a steak!

Preparation time: 1 hour and 10 minutes
Cooking time: 0 minutes
Servings: 6

Ingredients:

- 3 tablespoons salt
- 1 pound napa cabbage, chopped
- 1 carrot, julienned
- ½ cup daikon radish
- 3 green onion stalks, chopped
- 1 tablespoon fish sauce
- 3 tablespoons chili flakes
- 3 garlic cloves, minced
- 1 tablespoon sesame oil
- ½ inch ginger, grated

Directions:

6. In a bowl, mix cabbage with the salt, massage well for 10 minutes, cover and leave aside for 1 hour.
7. In a bowl, mix chili flakes with fish sauce, garlic, sesame oil and ginger and stir very well.
8. Drain cabbage well, rinses under cold water and transfer to a bowl.

9. Add carrots, green onions, radish and chili paste and stir everything.
10. Leave in a dark and cold place for at least 2 days before serving as a side for a keto steak.

Enjoy!

Nutrition: calories 60, fat 3, fiber 2, carbs 5, protein 1

Delicious Green Beans Side Dish

You will definitely enjoy this great side dish!

Preparation time: 10 minutes
Cooking time: 10 minutes
Servings: 4

Ingredients:

- 2/3 cup parmesan, grated
- 1 egg
- 12 ounces green beans
- Salt and black pepper to the taste
- ½ teaspoon garlic powder
- ¼ teaspoon paprika

Directions:

6. In a bowl, mix parmesan with salt, pepper, garlic powder and paprika and stir.
7. In another bowl, whisk the egg with salt and pepper.
8. Dredge green beans in egg and then in parmesan mix.
9. Place green beans on a lined baking sheet, introduce in the oven at 400 degrees F for 10 minutes.
10. Serve hot as a side dish.

Enjoy!

Nutrition: calories 114, fat 5, fiber 7, carbs 3, protein 9

Simple Cauliflower Mash

This simple Ketogenic mash goes with a meat based dish!

Preparation time: 10 minutes
Cooking time: 10 minutes
Servings: 2

Ingredients:

- ¼ cup sour cream
- 1 small cauliflower head, florets separated
- Salt and black pepper to the taste
- 2 tablespoons feta cheese, crumbled
- 2 tablespoons black olives, pitted and sliced

Directions:

4. Put water in a pot, add some salt, bring to a boil over medium heat, add florets, cook for 10 minutes, take off heat and drain.
5. Return cauliflower to the pot, add salt and black pepper to the taste and the sour cream and blend suing an immersion blender.
6. Add black olives and feta cheese, stir and serve as a side dish.

Enjoy!

Nutrition: calories 100, fat 4, fiber 2, carbs 3, protein 2

Delicious Portobello Mushrooms

These are simply the best! It's a great keto side dish!

Preparation time: 10 minutes
Cooking time: 10 minutes
Servings: 4

Ingredients:

- 12 ounces Portobello mushrooms, sliced
- Salt and black pepper to the taste
- ½ teaspoon basil, dried
- 2 tablespoons olive oil
- ½ teaspoon tarragon, dried
- ½ teaspoon rosemary, dried
- ½ teaspoon thyme, dried
- 2 tablespoons balsamic vinegar

Directions:

3. In a bowl, mix oil with vinegar, salt, pepper, rosemary, tarragon, basil and thyme and whisk well.
4. Add mushroom slices, toss to coat well, place them on your preheated grill over medium high heat, cook for 5 minutes on both sides and serve as a keto side dish.

Enjoy!

Nutrition: calories 80, fat 4, fiber 4, carbs 2, protein 4

Brussels Sprouts Side Dish

This is an Asian-style side dish you must try!

Preparation time: 10 minutes
Cooking time: 10 minutes
Servings: 4

Ingredients:
- 1 pound Brussels sprouts, trimmed and halved
- Salt and black pepper to the taste
- 1 teaspoon sesame seeds
- 1 tablespoon green onions, chopped
- 1 and ½ tablespoons sukrin gold syrup
- 1 tablespoon coconut aminos
- 2 tablespoons sesame oil
- 1 tablespoon sriracha

Directions:
4. In a bowl, mix sesame oil with coconut aminos, sriracha, syrup, salt and black pepper and whisk well.
5. Heat up a pan over medium high heat, add Brussels sprouts and cook them for 5 minutes on each side.
6. Add sesame oil mix, toss to coat, sprinkle sesame seeds and green onions, stir again and serve as a side dish.

Enjoy!

Nutrition: calories 110, fat 4, fiber 4, carbs 6, protein 4

Delicious Pesto

This keto pesto can be served with a tasty chicken dish!

Preparation time: 10 minutes
Cooking time: 0 minutes
Servings: 4

Ingredients:

- ½ cup olive oil
- 2 cups basil
- 1/3 cup pine nuts
- 1/3 cup parmesan cheese, grated
- 2 garlic cloves, chopped
- Salt and black pepper to the taste

Directions:

4. Put basil in your food processor, add pine nuts and garlic and blend very well.
5. Add parmesan, salt, pepper and the oil gradually and blend again until you obtain a paste.
6. Serve with chicken!

Enjoy!

Nutrition: calories 100, fat 7, fiber 3, carbs 1, protein 5

Brussels Sprouts And Bacon

You will love Brussels sprouts from now on!

Preparation time: 10 minutes
Cooking time: 30 minutes
Servings: 4

Ingredients:

- 8 bacon strips, chopped
- 1 pound Brussels sprouts, trimmed and halved
- Salt and black pepper to the taste
- A pinch of cumin, ground
- A pinch of red pepper, crushed
- 2 tablespoons extra virgin olive oil

Directions:
5. In a bowl, mix Brussels sprouts with salt, pepper, cumin, red pepper and oil and toss to coat.
6. Spread Brussels sprouts on a lined baking sheet, introduce in the oven at 375 degrees F and bake for 30 minutes.
7. Meanwhile, heat up a pan over medium heat, add bacon pieces and cook them until they become crispy.
8. Divide baked Brussels sprouts on plates, top with bacon and serve as a side dish right away.

Enjoy!

Nutrition: calories 256, fat 20, fiber 6, carbs 5, protein 15

Delicious Spinach Side Dish

This is very creamy and tasty!

Preparation time: 10 minutes
Cooking time: 15 minutes
Servings: 2

Ingredients:

- 2 garlic cloves, minced
- 8 ounces spinach leaves
- A drizzle of olive oil
- Salt and black pepper to the taste
- 4 tablespoons sour cream
- 1 tablespoon ghee
- 2 tablespoons parmesan cheese, grated

Directions:

5. Heat up a pan with the oil over medium heat, add spinach, stir and cook until it softens.
6. Add salt, pepper, ghee, parmesan and ghee, stir and cook for 4 minutes.
7. Add sour cream, stir and cook for 5 minutes more.
8. Divide between plates and serve as a side dish.

Enjoy!

Nutrition: calories 133, fat 10, fiber 4, carbs 4, protein 2

Amazing Avocado Fries

Try them as a side dish for a delicious steak!

Preparation time: 10 minutes
Cooking time: 5 minutes
Servings: 3

Ingredients:

- 3 avocados, pitted, peeled, halved and sliced
- 1 and ½ cups sunflower oil
- 1 and ½ cups almond meal
- A pinch of cayenne pepper
- Salt and black pepper to the taste

Directions:

7. In a bowl mix almond meal with salt, pepper and cayenne and stir.
8. In a second bowl, whisk eggs with a pinch of salt and pepper.
9. Dredge avocado pieces in egg and then in almond meal mix.
10. Heat up a pan with the oil over medium high heat, add avocado fries and cook them until they are golden.

11. Transfer to paper towels, drain grease and divide between plates.
12. Serve as a side dish.

Enjoy!

Nutrition: calories 450, fat 43, fiber 4, carbs 7, protein 17

Simple Roasted Cauliflower

This is so delicious and very easy to make at home! It's a great keto side dish!

Preparation time: 10 minutes
Cooking time: 25 minutes
Servings: 6

Ingredients:

- 1 cauliflower head, florets separated
- Salt and black pepper to the taste
- 1/3 cup parmesan, grated
- 1 tablespoon parsley, chopped
- 3 tablespoons olive oil
- 2 tablespoons extra virgin olive oil

Directions:

5. In a bowl, mix oil with garlic, salt, pepper and cauliflower florets.
6. Toss to coat well, spread this on a lined baking sheet, introduce in the oven at 450 degrees F and bake for 25 minutes, stirring halfway.

7. Add parmesan and parsley, stir and cook for 5 minutes more.
8. Divide between plates and serve as a keto side dish. Enjoy!

Nutrition: calories 118, fat 2, fiber 3, carbs 1, protein 6

Mushroom And Spinach Side Dish

This is an Italian style keto side dish worth trying as soon as possible!

Preparation time: 10 minutes
Cooking time: 10 minutes
Servings: 4

Ingredients:

- 10 ounces spinach leaves, chopped
- Salt and black pepper to the taste
- 14 ounces mushrooms, chopped
- 2 garlic cloves, minced
- A handful parsley, chopped
- 1 yellow onion, chopped
- 4 tablespoons olive oil
- 2 tablespoons balsamic vinegar

Directions:

6. Heat up a pan with the oil over medium high heat, add garlic and onion, stir and cook for 4 minutes.
7. Add mushrooms, stir and cook for 3 minutes more.
8. Add spinach, stir and cook for 3 minutes.

9. Add vinegar, salt and pepper, stir and cook for 1 minute more.
10. Add parsley, stir, divide between plates and serve hot as a side dish.

Enjoy!

Nutrition: calories 200, fat 4, fiber 6, carbs 2, protein 12

Delicious Okra And Tomatoes

This is very simple and easy to make! It's one of the best keto sides ever!

Preparation time: 10 minutes
Cooking time: 10 minutes
Servings: 6

Ingredients:

- 14 ounces canned stewed tomatoes, chopped
- Salt and black pepper to the taste
- 2 celery stalks, chopped
- 1 yellow onion, chopped
- 1 pound okra, sliced
- 2 bacon slices, chopped
- 1 small green bell peppers, chopped

Directions:

5. Heat up a pan over medium high heat, add bacon, stir, brown for a few minutes, transfer to paper towels and leave aside for now.

6. Heat up the pan again over medium heat, add okra, bell pepper, onion and celery, stir and cook for 2 minutes.
7. Add tomatoes, salt and pepper, stir and cook for 3 minutes.
8. Divide on plates, garnish with crispy bacon and serve.

Enjoy!

Nutrition: calories 100, fat 2, fiber 3, carbs 2, protein 6

Amazing Snap Peas And Mint

This side dish is not just a keto one! It's a simple and quick one as well!

Preparation time: 10 minutes
Cooking time: 5 minutes
Servings: 4

Ingredients:
- ¾ pound sugar snap peas, trimmed
- Salt and black pepper to the taste
- 1 tablespoon mint leaves, chopped
- 2 teaspoons olive oil
- 3 green onions, chopped
- 1 garlic clove, minced

Directions:
4. Heat up a pan with the oil over medium high heat.
5. Add snap peas, salt, pepper, green onions, garlic and mint.
6. Stir everything, cook for 5 minutes, divide between plates and serve as a side dish for a pork steak.

Enjoy!

Nutrition: calories 70, fat 1, fiber 1, carbs 0.4, protein 6

Collard Greens Side Dish

This is just unbelievably amazing!

Preparation time: 10 minutes
Cooking time: 2 hours and 15 minutes
Servings: 10

Ingredients:

- 5 bunches collard greens, chopped
- Salt and black pepper to the taste
- 1 tablespoon red pepper flakes, crushed
- 5 cups chicken stock
- 1 turkey leg
- 2 tablespoons garlic, minced
- ¼ cup olive oil

Directions:

6. Heat up a pot with the oil over medium heat, add garlic, stir and cook for 1 minute.
7. Add stock, salt, pepper and turkey leg, stir, cover and simmer for 30 minutes.
8. Add collard greens, cover pot again and cook for 45 minutes more.
9. Reduce heat to medium, add more salt and pepper, stir and cook for 1 hour.

10. Drain greens, mix them with red pepper flakes, stir, divide between plates and serve as a side dish.

Enjoy!

Nutrition: calories 143, fat 3, fiber 4, carbs 3, protein 6

Eggplant And Tomato Side Dish

It's a keto side dish you will make over and over again!

Preparation time: 10 minutes
Cooking time: 15 minutes
Servings: 4

Ingredients:

- 1 tomato, sliced
- 1 eggplant, sliced into thin rounds
- Salt and black pepper to the taste
- ¼ cup parmesan, grated
- A drizzle of olive oil

Directions:

5. Place eggplant slices on a lined baking dish, drizzle some oil and sprinkle half of the parmesan.
6. Top eggplant slices with tomato ones, season with salt and pepper to the taste and sprinkle the rest of the cheese over them.
7. Introduce in the oven at 400 degrees F and bake for 15 minutes.
8. Divide between plates and serve hot as a side dish.

Enjoy!

Nutrition: calories 55, fat 1, fiber 1, carbs 0.5, protein 7

Broccoli With Lemon Almond Butter

This side dish is perfect for a grilled steak!

Preparation time: 10 minutes
Cooking time: 10 minutes
Servings: 4

Ingredients:

- 1 broccoli head, florets separated
- Salt and black pepper to the taste
- ¼ cup almonds, blanched
- 1 teaspoon lemon zest
- ¼ cup coconut butter, melted
- 2 tablespoons lemon juice

Directions:

6. Put water in a pot, add salt and bring to a boil over medium high heat.
7. Place broccoli florets in a steamer basket, place into the pot, cover and steam for 8 minutes.
8. Drain and transfer to a bowl.

9. Heat up a pan with the coconut butter over medium heat, add lemon juice, lemon zest and almonds, stir and take off heat.
10. Add broccoli, toss to coat, divide between plates and serve as a Ketogenic side dish.

Enjoy!

Nutrition: calories 170, fat 15, fiber 4, carbs 4, protein 4

Simple Sautéed Broccoli

Serve this with some baked chicken or fish!

Preparation time: 10 minutes
Cooking time: 22 minutes
Servings: 4

Ingredients:

- 5 tablespoons olive oil
- 1 garlic clove, minced
- 1 pound broccoli florets
- 1 tablespoon parmesan, grated
- Salt and black pepper to the taste

Directions:

1. Put water in a pot, add salt, bring to a boil over medium high heat, add broccoli, cook for 5 minutes and drain.
2. Heat up a pan with the oil over medium high heat, add garlic, stir and cook for 2 minutes.
3. Add broccoli, stir and cook for 15 minutes.
4. Take off heat, sprinkle parmesan, divide between plates and serve.

Enjoy!

Nutrition: calories 193, fat 14, fiber 3, carbs 6, protein 5

Easy Grilled Onions

This Ketogenic side dish is perfect for a steak!

Preparation time: 10 minutes
Cooking time: 1 hour
Servings: 4

Ingredients:

- ½ cup ghee
- 4 onions
- 4 chicken bouillon cubes
- Salt and black pepper

Direction:

1. Cut onion tops make a hole in the middle, divide ghee and chicken bouillon cubes into these holes and season with salt and pepper.
2. Wrap onions in tin foil, place them on preheated kitchen grill and grill for 1 hour.
3. Unwrap onions, chop them into big chunks, arrange on plates and serve as a side dish.

Enjoy!

Nutrition: calories 135, fat 11, fiber 4, carbs 6, protein 3

Sautéed Zucchinis

Serve them with some chicken meat and enjoy a perfect meal!

Preparation time: 10 minutes
Cooking time: 15 minutes
Servings: 6

Ingredients:
- 1 red onion, chopped
- 1 tomato, chopped
- ½ pound tomatoes, chopped
- Salt and black pepper to the taste
- 1 garlic clove, minced
- 1 garlic clove, minced
- 1 teaspoon Italian seasoning
- 4 zucchinis, sliced

Directions:
1. Heat up a pan with the oil over medium heat, add onion, salt and pepper, stir and cook for 2 minutes.
2. Add mushrooms and zucchinis, stir and cook for 5 minutes.
3. Add garlic, tomatoes and Italian seasoning, stir, cook for 6 minutes more.
4. Take off heat, divide between plates and serve as a side dish.

Enjoy!

Nutrition: calories 70, fat 3, fiber 2, carbs 6, protein 4

Delicious Fried Swiss Chard

You must try this keto side dish! It goes perfectly with some grilled meat!

Preparation time: 10 minutes
Cooking time: 10 minutes
Servings: 2

Ingredients:

- 2 tablespoons ghee
- 4 bacon slices, chopped
- 1 bunch Swiss chard, roughly chopped
- ½ teaspoon garlic paste
- 3 tablespoons lemon juice
- Salt and black pepper to the taste

Directions:

1. Heat up a pan over medium heat, add bacon pieces and cook until it's crispy.
2. Add ghee and stir until it melts.
3. Add garlic paste and lemon juice, stir and cook for 1 minute.
4. Add Swiss chard, stir and cook for 4 minutes.
5. Add salt and black pepper to the taste, stir, divide between plates and serve as a keto side dish.

Enjoy!

Nutrition: calories 300, fat 32, fiber 7, carbs 6, protein 8

Delicious Side Mushroom Salad

This is really delicious and easy to make!

Preparation time: 10 minutes
Cooking time: 10 minutes
Servings: 4

Ingredients:

- 2 tablespoons ghee
- 1 pound cremini mushrooms, chopped
- 4 tablespoons extra virgin olive oil
- Salt and black pepper to the taste
- 4 bunches arugula
- 8 slices prosciutto
- 2 tablespoons apple cider vinegar
- 8 sun-dried tomatoes in oil, drained and chopped
- Some parmesan shavings
- Some parsley leaves, chopped

Directions:

1. Heat up a pan with the ghee and half of the oil over medium high heat.
2. Add mushrooms, salt and pepper, stir and cook for 3 minutes.
3. Reduce heat, stir again and cook for 3 more minutes.

4. Add the rest of the oil and the vinegar, stir and cook 1 minute more
5. Place arugula on a serving platter, add prosciutto on top, add mushroom mix, sun dried tomatoes, more salt and pepper, parmesan shavings and parsley and serve.

Enjoy!

Nutrition: calories 160, fat 4, fiber 2, carbs 2, protein 6

Greek Side Salad

Get ready for a fabulous combination of ingredients! Taste this amazing salad at once!

Preparation time: 10 minutes
Cooking time: 7 minutes
Servings: 6

Ingredients:

- ½ pounds mushrooms, sliced
- 1 tablespoon extra virgin olive oil
- 3 garlic cloves, minced
- 1 teaspoon basil, dried
- Salt and black pepper to the taste
- 1 tomato, diced
- 3 tablespoons lemon juice
- ½ cup water
- 1 tablespoons coriander, chopped

Directions:

1. Heat up a pan with the oil over medium heat, add mushrooms, stir and cook for 3 minutes.
2. Add basil and garlic, stir and cook for 1 minute more.
3. Add water, salt, pepper, tomato and lemon juice, stir and cook for a few minutes more.

4. Take off heat, transfer to a bowl, leave aside to cool down, sprinkle coriander and serve.

Enjoy!

Nutrition: calories 200, fat 2, fiber 2, carbs 1, protein 10

Delicious Veal Stew

No matter how busy you are, you can make the time to prepare this keto dish!

Preparation time: 10 minutes
Cooking time: 2 hours and 10 minutes
Servings: 12

Ingredients:
- 2 tablespoons avocado oil
- 3 pounds veal, cubed
- 1 yellow onion, chopped
- 1 small garlic clove, minced
- Salt and black pepper to the taste
- 1 cup water
- 1 and ½ cups marsala wine
- 10 ounces canned tomato paste
- 1 carrot, chopped
- 7 ounces mushrooms, chopped
- 3 egg yolks
- ½ cup heavy cream
- 2 teaspoons oregano, dried

Directions:
1. Heat up a pot with the oil over medium high heat, add veal, stir and brown it for a few minutes.
2. Add garlic and onion, stir and cook for 2-3 minutes more.
3. Add wine, water, oregano, tomato paste, mushrooms, carrots, salt and pepper, stir, bring to a boil, cover, reduce heat to low and cook for 1 hour and 45 minutes.
4. In a bowl, mix cream with egg yolks and whisk well.
5. Pour this into the pot, stir, cook for 15 minutes more, add more salt and pepper if needed, divide into bowls and serve.

Enjoy!

Nutrition: calories 254, fat 15, fiber 1, carbs 3, protein 23

Veal And Tomatoes Dish

Make a special dinner for your loved ones! Try this keto recipe!

Preparation time: 10 minutes
Cooking time: 40 minutes
Servings: 4

Ingredients:
- 4 medium veal leg steaks
- A drizzle of avocado oil
- 2 garlic cloves, minced
- 1 red onion, chopped
- Salt and black pepper to the taste
- 2 teaspoons sage, chopped
- 15 ounces canned tomatoes, chopped
- 2 tablespoons parsley, chopped
- 1 ounce bocconcini, sliced
- Green beans, steamed for serving

Directions:
1. Heat up a pan with the oil over medium high heat, add veal, cook for 2 minutes on each side and transfer to a baking dish.
2. Return pan to heat, add onion, stir and cook for 4 minutes.
3. Add sage and garlic, stir and cook for 1 minute.
4. Add tomatoes, stir, bring to a boil and cook for 10 minutes.
5. Pour this over veal, add bocconcini and parsley, introduce in the oven at 350 degrees G and bake for 20 minutes.
6. Divide between plates and serve with steamed green beans on the side.

Enjoy!

Nutrition: calories 276, fat 6, fiber 4, carbs 5, protein 36

Veal Parmesan

It's a very popular keto dish and you should learn how to make it!

Preparation time: 10 minutes
Cooking time: 1 hour and 10 minutes
Servings: 6

Ingredients:

- 8 veal cutlets
- 2/3 cup parmesan, grated
- 8 provolone cheese slices
- Salt and black pepper to the taste
- 5 cups tomato sauce
- A pinch of garlic salt
- Cooking spray
- 2 tablespoons ghee
- 2 tablespoons coconut oil, melted
- 1 teaspoon Italian seasoning

Directions:

1. Season veal cutlets with salt, pepper and garlic salt,
2. Heat up a pan with the ghee and the oil over medium high heat, add veal and cook until they brown on all sides.
3. Spread half of the tomato sauce on the bottom of a baking dish which you've greased with some cooking spray.
4. Add veal cutlets, then sprinkle Italian seasoning and spread the rest of the sauce.
5. Cover dish, introduce in the oven at 350 degrees F and bake for 40 minutes.

6. Uncover dish, spread provolone cheese and sprinkle parmesan, introduce in the oven again and bake for 15 minutes more.
7. Divide between plates and serve.

Enjoy!

Nutrition: calories 362, fat 21, fiber 2, carbs 6, protein 26

Veal Piccata

Make this for your loved one tonight!

Preparation time: 10 minutes
Cooking time: 15 minutes
Servings: 2

Ingredients:
- 2 tablespoons ghee
- ¼ cup white wine
- ¼ cup chicken stock
- 1 and ½ tablespoons capers
- 1 garlic clove, minced
- 8 ounces veal scallops
- Salt and black pepper to the taste

Directions:
1. Heat up a pan with half of the butter over medium high heat, add veal cutlets, season with salt and pepper, cook for 1 minute on each side and transfer to a plate.
2. Heat up the pan again over medium heat, add garlic, stir and cook for 1 minute.
3. Add wine, stir and simmer for 2 minutes.
4. Add stock, capers, salt, pepper, the rest of the ghee and return veal to pan.
5. Stir everything, cover pan and cook piccata on medium low heat until veal is tender.

Enjoy!

Nutrition: calories 204, fat 12, fiber 1, carbs 5, protein 10

Delicious Roasted Sausage

It's very easy to make at home tonight!

Preparation time: 10 minutes
Cooking time: 1 hour
Servings: 6

Ingredients:
- 3 red bell peppers, chopped
- 2 pounds Italian pork sausage, sliced
- Salt and black pepper to the taste
- 2 pounds Portobello mushrooms, sliced
- 2 sweet onions, chopped
- 1 tablespoon swerve
- A drizzle of olive oil

Directions:
1. In a baking dish, mix sausage slices with oil, salt, pepper, bell pepper, mushrooms, onion and swerve.
2. Toss to coat, introduce in the oven at 300 degrees F and bake for 1 hour.
3. Divide between plates and serve hot.

Enjoy!

Nutrition: calories 130, fat 12, fiber 1, carbs 3, protein 9

Baked Sausage And Kale

This keto dish will be ready in 20 minutes!

Preparation time: 5 minutes
Cooking time: 30 minutes
Servings: 4

Ingredients:

- 1 cup yellow onion, chopped
- 1 and ½ pound Italian pork sausage, sliced
- ½ cup red bell pepper, chopped
- Salt and black pepper to the taste
- 5 pounds kale, chopped
- 1 teaspoon garlic, minced
- ¼ cup red hot chili pepper, chopped
- 1 cup water

Directions:

1. Heat up a pan over medium high heat, add sausage, stir, reduce heat to medium and cook for 10 minutes.
2. Add onions, stir and cook for 3-4 minutes more.
3. Add bell pepper and garlic, stir and cook for 1 minute.
4. Add kale, chili pepper, salt, pepper and water, stir and cook for 10 minutes more.
5. Divide between plates and serve.

Enjoy!

Nutrition: calories 150, fat 4, fiber 1, carbs 2, protein 12

Sausage With Tomatoes And Cheese

It's a surprising and very tasty combination!

Preparation time: 10 minutes
Cooking time: 30 minutes
Servings: 4

Ingredients:
- 2 ounces coconut oil, melted
- 2 pounds Italian pork sausage, chopped
- 1 onion, sliced
- 4 sun-dried tomatoes, thinly sliced
- Salt and black pepper to the taste
- ½ pound gouda cheese, grated
- 3 yellow bell peppers, chopped
- 3 orange bell peppers, chopped
- A pinch of red pepper flakes
- A handful parsley, thinly sliced

Directions:
1. Heat up a pan with the oil over medium high heat, add sausage slices, stir, cook for 3 minutes on each side, transfer to a plate and leave aside for now.
2. Heat up the pan again over medium heat, add onion, yellow and orange bell peppers and tomatoes, stir and cook for 5 minutes.
3. Add pepper flakes, salt and pepper, stir well, cook for 1 minute and take off heat.

4. Arrange sausage slices into a baking dish, add bell peppers mix on top, add parsley and gouda as well, introduce in the oven at 350 degrees F and bake for 15 minutes.
5. Divide between plates and serve hot.

Enjoy!

Nutrition: calories 200, fat 5, fiber 3, carbs 6, protein 14

Delicious Sausage Salad
Check this out! It's very tasty!

Preparation time: 10 minutes
Cooking time: 7 minutes
Servings: 4

Ingredients:
- 8 pork sausage links, sliced
- 1 pound mixed cherry tomatoes, cut in halves
- 4 cups baby spinach
- 1 tablespoon avocado oil
- 1 pound mozzarella cheese, cubed
- 2 tablespoons lemon juice
- 2/3 cup basil pesto
- Salt and black pepper to the taste

Directions:
1. Heat up a pan with the oil over medium high heat, add sausage slices, stir and cook them for 4 minutes on each side.
2. Meanwhile, in a salad bowl, mix spinach with mozzarella, tomatoes, salt, pepper, lemon juice and pesto and toss to coat.
3. Add sausage pieces, toss again and serve.

Enjoy!

Nutrition: calories 250, fat 12, fiber 3, carbs 8, protein 18

Delicious Sausage And Peppers Soup

This keto soup will hypnotize everyone!

Preparation time: 10 minutes
Cooking time: 1 hour and 10 minutes
Servings: 6

Ingredients:
- 1 tablespoon avocado oil
- 32 ounces pork sausage meat
- 10 ounces canned tomatoes and jalapenos, chopped
- 10 ounces spinach
- 1 green bell pepper, chopped
- 4 cups beef stock
- 1 teaspoon onion powder
- Salt and black pepper to the taste
- 1 tablespoon cumin
- 1 tablespoon chili powder
- 1 teaspoon garlic powder
- 1 teaspoon Italian seasoning

Directions:
1. Heat up a pot with the oil over medium heat, add sausage, stir and brown for a couple of minutes on all sides.
2. Add green bell pepper, salt and pepper, stir and cook for 3 minutes.
3. Add tomatoes and jalapenos, stir and cook for 2 minutes more.
4. Add spinach, stir, cover and cook for 7 minutes.
5. Add stock, onion powder, garlic powder, chili powder, cumin, salt, pepper and Italian seasoning, stir everything, cover pot and cook for 30 minutes.
6. Uncover pot and cook soup for 15 minutes more.
7. Divide into bowls and serve.

Enjoy!

Nutrition: calories 524, fat 43, fiber 2, carbs 4, protein 26

Italian Sausage Soup

Everyone can make this amazing keto soup! It's so tasty and healthy!

Preparation time: 10 minutes
Cooking time: 30 minutes
Servings: 12

Ingredients:

- 64 ounces chicken stock
- A drizzle of avocado oil
- 1 cup heavy cream
- 10 ounces spinach
- 6 bacon slices, chopped
- 1 pound radishes, chopped
- 2 garlic cloves, minced
- Salt and black pepper to the taste
- A pinch of red pepper flakes, crushed
- 1 yellow onion, chopped
- 1 and ½ pounds hot pork sausage, chopped

Directions:

1. Heat up a pot with a drizzle of avocado oil over medium high heat, add sausage, onion and garlic, stir and brown for a few minutes.
2. Add stock, spinach and radishes, stir and bring to a simmer.
3. Add bacon, cream, salt, pepper and red pepper flakes, stir and cook for 20 minutes more.
4. Divide into bowls and serve.

Enjoy!

Nutrition: calories 291, fat 22, fiber 2, carbs 4, protein 17

Amazing Broccoli And Cauliflower Cream

This is so textured and delicious!

Preparation time: 10 minutes
Cooking time: 15 minutes
Servings: 5

Ingredients:
- 1 cauliflower head, florets separated
- 1 broccoli head, florets separated
- Salt and black pepper to the taste
- 2 garlic cloves, minced
- 2 bacon slices, chopped
- 2 tablespoons ghee

Directions:
1. Heat up a pot with the ghee over medium high heat, add garlic and bacon, stir and cook for 3 minutes.
2. Add cauliflower and broccoli florets, stir and cook for 2 minutes more.
3. Add water to cover them, cover pot and simmer for 10 minutes.
4. Add salt and pepper, stir again and blend soup using an immersion blender.
5. Simmer for a couple more minutes over medium heat, ladle into bowls and serve.

Enjoy!

Nutrition: calories 230, fat 3, fiber 3, carbs 6, protein 10

Broccoli Stew

This veggie stew is just delicious!

Preparation time: 10 minutes
Cooking time: 40 minutes
Servings: 4

Ingredients:
- 1 broccoli head, florets separated
- 2 teaspoons coriander seeds
- A drizzle of olive oil
- 1 yellow onion, chopped
- Salt and black pepper to the taste
- A pinch of red pepper, crushed
- 1 small ginger piece, chopped
- 1 garlic clove, minced
- 28 ounces canned tomatoes, pureed

Directions:
1. Put water in a pot, add salt, bring to a boil over medium high heat, add broccoli florets, steam them for 2 minutes, transfer them to a bowl filled with ice water, drain them and leave aside.
2. Heat up a pan over medium high heat, add coriander seeds, toast them for 4 minutes, transfer to a grinder, ground them and leave aside as well.
3. Heat up a pot with the oil over medium heat, add onions, salt, pepper and red pepper, stir and cook for 7 minutes.

4. Add ginger, garlic and coriander seeds, stir and cook for 3 minutes.
5. Add tomatoes, bring to a boil and simmer for 10 minutes.
6. Add broccoli, stir and cook your stew for 12 minutes.
7. Divide into bowls and serve.

Enjoy!

Nutrition: calories 150, fat 4, fiber 2, carbs 5, protein 12

Amazing Watercress Soup

A Chinese style keto soup sounds pretty amazing, doesn't it?

Preparation time: 10 minutes
Cooking time: 10 minutes
Servings: 4

Ingredients:
- 6 cup chicken stock
- ¼ cup sherry
- 2 teaspoons coconut aminos
- 6 and ½ cups watercress
- Salt and black pepper to the taste
- 2 teaspoons sesame seed
- 3 shallots, chopped
- 3 egg whites, whisked

Directions:
1. Put stock into a pot, mix with salt, pepper, sherry and coconut aminos, stir and bring to a boil over medium high heat.
2. Add shallots, watercress and egg whites, stir, bring to a boil, divide into bowls and serve with sesame seeds sprinkled on top.

Enjoy!

Nutrition: calories 50, fat 1, fiber 0, carbs 1, protein 5

Delicious Bok Choy Soup

You can even have this for dinner!

Preparation time: 10 minutes
Cooking time: 15 minutes
Servings: 4

Ingredients:
- 3 cups beef stock
- 1 yellow onion, chopped
- 1 bunch bok choy, chopped
- 1 and ½ cups mushrooms, chopped
- Salt and black pepper to the taste
- ½ tablespoon red pepper flakes
- 3 tablespoons coconut aminos
- 3 tablespoons parmesan, grated
- 2 tablespoons Worcestershire sauce
- 2 bacon strips, chopped

Directions:
1. Heat up a pot over medium high heat, add bacon, stir, cook until it until it's crispy, transfer to paper towels and drain grease.
2. Heat up the pot again over medium heat, add mushrooms and onions, stir and cook for 5 minutes.
3. Add stock, bok choy, coconut aminos, salt, pepper, pepper flakes and Worcestershire sauce, stir, cover and cook until bok choy is tender.
4. Ladle soup into bowls, sprinkle parmesan and bacon and serve.

Enjoy!

Nutrition: calories 100, fat 3, fiber 1, carbs 2, protein 6

Bok Choy Stir Fry

It's simple, it's easy and very delicious!

Preparation time: 10 minutes
Cooking time: 7 minutes
Servings: 2

Ingredients:
- 2 garlic cloves, minced
- 2 cup bok choy, chopped
- 2 bacon slices, chopped
- Salt and black pepper to the taste
- A drizzle of avocado oil

Directions:
1. Heat up a pan with the oil over medium heat, add bacon, stir and brown until it's crispy, transfer to paper towels and drain grease.
2. Return pan to medium heat, add garlic and bok choy, stir and cook for 4 minutes.
3. Add salt, pepper and return bacon, stir, cook for 1 minute more, divide between plates and serve.

Enjoy!

Nutrition: calories 50, fat 1, fiber 1, carbs 2, protein 2

Cream Of Celery

This will impress you!

Preparation time: 10 minutes
Cooking time: 40 minutes
Servings: 4

Ingredients:
- 1 bunch celery, chopped
- Salt and black pepper to the taste
- 3 bay leaves
- ½ garlic head, chopped
- 2 yellow onions, chopped
- 4 cups chicken stock
- ¾ cup heavy cream
- 2 tablespoons ghee

Directions:
1. Heat up a pot with the ghee over medium high heat, add onions, salt and pepper, stir and cook for 5 minutes.
2. Add bay leaves, garlic and celery, stir and cook for 15 minutes.
3. Add stock, more salt and pepper, stir, cover pot, reduce heat and simmer for 20 minutes.
4. Add cream, stir and blend everything using an immersion blender.
5. Ladle into soup bowls and serve.

Enjoy!

Nutrition: calories 150, fat 3, fiber 1, carbs 2, protein 6

Delightful Celery Soup

It's so delightful and delicious! Try it!

Preparation time: 10 minutes
Cooking time: 25 minutes
Servings: 8

Ingredients:
- 26 ounces celery leaves and stalks, chopped
- 1 tablespoon onion flakes
- Salt and black pepper to the taste
- 3 teaspoons fenugreek powder
- 3 teaspoons veggie stock powder
- 10 ounces sour cream

Directions:
1. Put celery into a pot, add water to cover, add onion flakes, salt, pepper, stock powder and fenugreek powder, stir, bring to a boil over medium heat and simmer for 20 minutes.
2. Use an immersion blender to make your cream, add sour cream, more salt and pepper and blend again.
3. Heat up soup again over medium heat, ladle into bowls and serve.

Enjoy!

Nutrition: calories 140, fat 2, fiber 1, carbs 5, protein 10

Amazing Celery Stew

This Iranian style keto stew is so tasty and easy to make!

Preparation time: 10 minutes
Cooking time: 30 minutes
Servings: 6

Ingredients:
- 1 celery bunch, roughly chopped
- 1 yellow onion, chopped
- 1 bunch green onion, chopped
- 4 garlic cloves, minced
- Salt and black pepper to the taste
- 1 parsley bunch, chopped
- 2 mint bunches, chopped
- 3 dried Persian lemons, pricked with a fork
- 2 cups water
- 2 teaspoons chicken bouillon
- 4 tablespoons olive oil

Directions:
1. Heat up a pot with the oil over medium high heat, add onion, green onions and garlic, stir and cook for 6 minutes.
2. Add celery, Persian lemons, chicken bouillon, salt, pepper and water, stir, cover pot and simmer on medium heat for 20 minutes.
3. Add parsley and mint, stir and cook for 10 minutes more.
4. Divide into bowls and serve.

Enjoy!

Nutrition: calories 170, fat 7, fiber 4, carbs 6, protein 10

Spinach Soup

It's a textured and creamy keto soup you have to try soon!

Preparation time: 10 minutes
Cooking time: 15 minutes
Servings: 8

Ingredients:
- 2 tablespoons ghee
- 20 ounces spinach, chopped
- 1 teaspoon garlic, minced
- Salt and black pepper to the taste
- 45 ounces chicken stock
- ½ teaspoon nutmeg, ground
- 2 cups heavy cream
- 1 yellow onion, chopped

Directions:
1. Heat up a pot with the ghee over medium heat, add onion, stir and cook for 4 minutes.
2. Add garlic, stir and cook for 1 minute.
3. Add spinach and stock, stir and cook for 5 minutes.
4. Blend soup with an immersion blender and heat up the soup again.
5. Add salt, pepper, nutmeg and cream, stir and cook for 5 minutes more.
6. Ladle into bowls and serve.

Enjoy!

Nutrition: calories 245, fat 24, fiber 3, carbs 4, protein 6

Delicious Mustard Greens Sauté
This is so tasty!

Preparation time: 10 minutes
Cooking time: 20 minutes
Servings: 4

Ingredients:
- 2 garlic cloves, minced
- 1 tablespoon olive oil
- 2 and ½ pounds collard greens, chopped
- 1 teaspoon lemon juice
- 1 tablespoon ghee
- Salt and black pepper to the taste

Directions:
1. Put some water in a pot, add salt and bring to a simmer over medium heat.
2. Add greens, cover and cook for 15 minutes.
3. Drain collard greens well, press out liquid and put them into a bowl.
4. Heat up a pan with the oil and the ghee over medium high heat, add collard greens, salt, pepper and garlic.
5. Stir well and cook for 5 minutes.
6. Add more salt and pepper if needed, drizzle lemon juice, stir, divide between plates and serve.

Enjoy!

Nutrition: calories 151, fat 6, fiber 3, carbs 7, protein 8

Tasty Collards Greens And Ham

This tasty dish will be ready in not time!

Preparation time: 10 minutes
Cooking time: 1 hour and 40 minutes
Servings: 4

Ingredients:
- 4 ounces ham, boneless, cooked and chopped
- 1 tablespoon olive oil
- 2 pounds collard greens, cut in medium strips
- 1 teaspoon red pepper flakes, crushed
- Salt and black pepper to the taste
- 2 cups chicken stock
- 1 yellow onion, chopped
- 4 ounces dry white wine
- 1 ounce salt pork
- ¼ cup apple cider vinegar
- ½ cup ghee, melted

Directions:
1. Heat up a pan with the oil over medium high heat, add ham and onion, stir and cook for 4 minutes.
2. Add salt pork, collard greens, stock, vinegar and wine, stir and bring to a boil.
3. Reduce heat, cover pan and cook for 1 hour and 30 minutes stirring from time to time.
4. Add ghee, discard salt pork, stir, cook everything for 10 minutes, divide between plates and serve.

Enjoy!

Nutrition: calories 150, fat 12, fiber 2, carbs 4, protein 8

Tasty Collard Greens And Tomatoes
This is just fantastic!

Preparation time: 10 minutes
Cooking time: 12 minutes
Servings: 5

Ingredients:
- 1 pound collard greens
- 3 bacon strips, chopped
- ¼ cup cherry tomatoes, halved
- 1 tablespoon apple cider vinegar
- 2 tablespoons chicken stock
- Salt and black pepper to the taste

Directions:
1. Heat up a pan over medium heat, add bacon, stir and cook until it browns.
2. Add tomatoes, collard greens, vinegar, stock, salt and pepper, stir and cook for 8 minutes.
3. Add more salt and pepper, stir again gently, divide between plates and serve.

Enjoy!

Nutrition: calories 120, fat 8, fiber 1, carbs 3, protein 7

Simple Mustard Greens Dish

Everyone can make this simple keto dish! You'll see!

Preparation time: 5 minutes
Cooking time: 15 minutes
Servings: 4

Ingredients:
- 2 garlic cloves, minced
- 1 pound mustard greens, torn
- 1 tablespoon olive oil
- ½ cup yellow onion, sliced
- Salt and black pepper to the taste
- 3 tablespoons veggie stock
- ¼ teaspoon dark sesame oil

Directions:
1. Heat up a pan with the oil over medium heat, add onions, stir and brown them for 10 minutes.
2. Add garlic, stir and cook for 1 minute.
3. Add stock, greens, salt and pepper, stir and cook for 5 minutes more.
4. Add more salt and pepper and the sesame oil, toss to coat, divide between plates and serve.

Enjoy!

Nutrition: calories 120, fat 3, fiber 1, carbs 3, protein 6

Delicious Collard Greens And Poached Eggs
This will really make everyone love your cooking!

Preparation time: 10 minutes
Cooking time: 15 minutes
Servings: 6

Ingredients:
- 1 tablespoon chipotle in adobo, mashed
- 6 eggs
- 3 tablespoons ghee
- 1 yellow onion, chopped
- 2 garlic cloves, minced
- 6 bacon slices, chopped
- 3 bunches collard greens, chopped
- ½ cup chicken stock
- Salt and black pepper to the taste
- 1 tablespoon lime juice
- Some grated cheddar cheese

Directions:
1. Heat up a pan over medium high heat, add bacon, cook until it's crispy, transfer to paper towels, drain grease and leave aside.
2. Heat up the pan again over medium heat, add garlic and onion, stir and cook for 2 minutes.
3. Return bacon to the pan, stir and cook for 3 minutes more.
4. Add chipotle in adobo paste, collard greens, salt and pepper, stir and cook for 10 minutes.

5. Add stock and lime juice and stir.
6. Make 6 holes in collard greens mix, divide ghee in them, crack an egg in each hole, cover pan and cook until eggs are done.
7. Divide this between plates and serve with cheddar cheese sprinkled on top.

Enjoy!

Nutrition: calories 245, fat 20, fiber 1, carbs 5, protein 12

Collard Greens Soup

This is a keto soup even vegetarians will love!

Preparation time: 10 minutes
Cooking time: 40 minutes
Servings: 12

Ingredients:
- 1 teaspoon chili powder
- 1 tablespoon avocado oil
- 2 teaspoons smoked paprika
- 1 teaspoon cumin
- 1 yellow onion, chopped
- A pinch of red pepper flakes
- 10 cups water
- 3 celery stalks, chopped
- 3 carrots, chopped
- 15 ounces canned tomatoes, chopped
- 2 tablespoons tamari sauce
- 6 ounces canned tomato paste
- 2 tablespoons lemon juice
- Salt and black pepper to the taste
- 6 cups collard greens, stems discarded
- 1 tablespoon swerve
- 1 teaspoon garlic granules
- 1 tablespoon herb seasoning

Directions:
1. Heat up a pot with the oil over medium high heat, add cumin, pepper flakes, paprika and chili powder and stir well.
2. Add celery, onion and carrots, stir and cook for 10 minutes.
3. Add tamari sauce, tomatoes, tomato paste, water, lemon juice, salt, pepper, herb seasoning, swerve, garlic granules and collard greens, stir, bring to a boil, cover and cook for 30 minutes.
4. Stir again, ladle into bowls and serve.

Enjoy!

Nutrition: calories 150, fat 3, fiber 2, carbs 4, protein 8

Spring Green Soup

This is a fresh spring Ketogenic soup!

Preparation time: 10 minutes
Cooking time: 30 minutes
Servings: 4

Ingredients:
- 2 cups mustard greens, chopped
- 2 cups collard greens, chopped
- 3 quarts veggie stock
- 1 yellow onion, chopped
- Salt and black pepper to the taste
- 2 tablespoons coconut aminos
- 2 teaspoons ginger, grated

Directions:
1. Put the stock into a pot and bring to a simmer over medium high heat.
2. Add mustard and collard greens, onion, salt, pepper, coconut aminos and ginger, stir, cover pot and cook for 30 minutes.
3. Blend soup using an immersion blender, add more salt and pepper, heat up over medium heat, ladle into soup bowls and serve.

Enjoy!

Nutrition: calories 140, fat 2, fiber 1, carbs 3, protein 7

Mustard Greens And Spinach Soup

This Indian style keto soup is amazing!

Preparation time: 10 minutes
Cooking time: 15 minutes
Servings: 6

Ingredients:
- ½ teaspoon fenugreek seeds
- 1 teaspoon cumin seeds
- 1 tablespoon avocado oil
- 1 teaspoon coriander seeds
- 1 cup yellow onion, chopped
- 1 tablespoon garlic, minced
- 1 tablespoon ginger, grated
- ½ teaspoon turmeric, ground
- 5 cups mustard greens, chopped
- 3 cups coconut milk
- 1 tablespoon jalapeno, chopped
- 5 cups spinach, torn
- Salt and black pepper to the taste
- 2 teaspoons ghee
- ½ teaspoon paprika

Directions:
1. Heat up a pot with the oil over medium high heat, add coriander, fenugreek and cumin seeds, stir and brown them for 2 minutes.
2. Add onions, stir and cook for 3 minutes more.
3. Add half of the garlic, jalapenos, ginger and turmeric, stir and cook for 3 minutes more.
4. Add mustard greens and spinach, stir and sauté everything for 10 minutes.

5. Add milk, salt and pepper and blend soup using an immersion blender.
6. Heat up a pan with the ghee over medium heat, add garlic and paprika, stir well and take off heat.
7. Heat up the soup over medium heat, ladle into soup bowls, drizzle ghee and paprika all over and soup.

Enjoy!

Nutrition: calories 143, fat 6, fiber 3, carbs 7, protein 7

Roasted Asparagus

It's incredibly easy and super delicious!

Preparation time: 10 minutes
Cooking time: 10 minutes
Servings: 3

Ingredients:
- 1 asparagus bunch, trimmed
- 3 teaspoons avocado oil
- A splash of lemon juice
- Salt and black pepper to the taste
- 1 tablespoon oregano, chopped

Directions:
1. Spread asparagus spears on a lined baking sheet, season with salt and pepper, drizzle oil and lemon juice, sprinkle oregano and toss to coat well.
2. Introduce in the oven at 425 degrees F and bake for 10 minutes.
Divide between plates and serve.

Enjoy!

Nutrition: calories 130, fat 1, fiber 1, carbs 2, protein 3

Simple Asparagus Fries
These will be ready in only 10 minutes!

Preparation time: 10 minutes
Cooking time: 10 minutes
Servings: 2

Ingredients:
- ¼ cup parmesan, grated
- 16 asparagus spears, trimmed
- 1 egg, whisked
- ½ teaspoon onion powder
- 2 ounces pork rinds

Directions:
1. Crush pork rinds and put them in a bowl.
2. Add onion powder and cheese and stir everything.
3. Roll asparagus spears in egg, then dip them in pork rind mix and arrange them all on a lined baking sheet.
4. Introduce in the oven at 425 degrees F and bake for 10 minutes.
5. Divide between plates and serve them with some sour cream on the side.

Enjoy!

Nutrition: calories 120, fat 2, fiber 2, carbs 5, protein 8

Amazing Asparagus And Browned Butter

This keto dish is very delicious and it also looks wonderful!

Preparation time: 10 minutes
Cooking time: 15 minutes
Servings: 4

Ingredients:
- 5 ounces butter
- 1 tablespoon avocado oil
- 1 and ½ pounds asparagus, trimmed
- 1 and ½ tablespoons lemon juice
- A pinch of cayenne pepper
- 8 tablespoons sour cream
- Salt and black pepper to the taste
- 3 ounces parmesan, grated
- 4 eggs

Directions:
1. Heat up a pan with 2 ounces butter over medium high heat, add eggs, some salt and pepper, stir and scramble them.
2. Transfer eggs to a blender, add parmesan, sour cream, salt, pepper and cayenne pepper and blend everything well.
3. Heat up a pan with the oil over medium high heat, add asparagus, salt and pepper, roast for a few minutes, transfer to a plate and leave them aside.

4. Heat up the pan again with the rest of the butter over medium high heat, stir until it's brown, take off heat, add lemon juice and stir well.
5. Heat up the butter again, return asparagus, toss to coat, heat up well and divide between plates.
6. Add blended eggs on top and serve.

Enjoy!

Nutrition: calories 160, fat 7, fiber 2, carbs 6, protein 10

Delicious Doughnuts

These keto doughnuts look and taste wonderful!

Preparation time: 10 minutes
Cooking time: 15 minutes
Servings: 24

Ingredients:
- ¼ cup erythritol
- ¼ cup flaxseed meal
- ¾ cup almond flour
- 1 teaspoon baking powder
- 1 teaspoon vanilla extract
- 2 eggs
- 3 tablespoons coconut oil
- ¼ cup coconut milk
- 20 drops red food coloring
- A pinch of salt
- 1 tablespoon cocoa powder

Directions:
1. In a bowl, mix flaxseed meal with almond flour, cocoa powder, baking powder, erythritol and salt and stir.
2. In another bowl, mix coconut oil with coconut milk, vanilla, food coloring and eggs and stir.
3. Combine the 2 mixtures, stir using a hand mixer, transfer to a bag, make a hole in the bag and shape 12 doughnuts on a baking sheet.
4. Introduce in the oven at 350 degrees F and bake for 15 minutes.
5. Arrange them on a platter and serve them.

Enjoy!

Nutrition: calories 60, fat 4, fiber 0, carbs 1, protein 2

Chocolate Bombs

You must try these today!

Preparation time: 10 minutes
Cooking time: 10 minutes
Servings: 12

Ingredients:
- 10 tablespoons coconut oil
- 3 tablespoons macadamia nuts, chopped
- 2 packets stevia
- 5 tablespoons unsweetened coconut powder
- A pinch of salt

Directions:
1. Put coconut oil in a pot and melt over medium heat.
2. Add stevia, salt and cocoa powder, stir well and take off heat.
3. Spoon this into a candy tray and keep in the fridge for a while.
4. Sprinkle macadamia nuts on top and keep in the fridge until you serve them.

Enjoy!

Nutrition: calories 50, fat 1, fiber 0, carbs 1, protein 2

Amazing Jello Dessert
It's more than you can imagine!

Preparation time: 2 hours 10 minutes
Cooking time: 5 minutes
Servings: 12

Ingredients:
- 2 ounces packets sugar free jello
- 1 cup cold water
- 1 cup hot water
- 3 tablespoons erythritol
- 2 tablespoons gelatin powder
- 1 teaspoon vanilla extract
- 1 cup heavy cream
- 1 cup boiling water

Directions:
1. Put jello packets in a bowl, add 1 cup hot water, stir until it dissolves and then mix with 1 cup cold water.
2. Pour this into a lined square dish and keep in the fridge for 1 hour.
3. Cut into cubes and leave aside for now.
4. Meanwhile, in a bowl, mix erythritol with vanilla extract, 1 cup boiling water, gelatin and heavy cream and stir very well.
5. Pour half of this mix into a silicon round mold, spread jello cubes, then top with the rest of the gelatin.
6. Keep in the fridge for 1 more hour and then serve.

Enjoy!

Nutrition: calories 70, fat 1, fiber 0, carbs 1, protein 2

Strawberry Pie
It's so delicious!

Preparation time: 2 hours and 10 minutes
Cooking time: 5 minutes
Servings: 12

Ingredients:
For the crust:
- 1 cup coconut, shredded
- 1 cup sunflower seeds
- ¼ cup butter
- A pinch of salt

For the filling:
- 1 teaspoon gelatin
- 8 ounces cream cheese
- 4 ounces strawberries
- 2 tablespoons water
- ½ tablespoon lemon juice
- ¼ teaspoon stevia
- ½ cup heavy cream
- 8 ounces strawberries, chopped for serving
- 16 ounces heavy cream for serving

Directions:
1. In your food processor, mix sunflower seeds with coconut, a pinch of salt and butter and stir well.
2. Put this into a greased spring form pan and press well on the bottom.
3. Heat up a pan with the water over medium heat, add gelatin, stir until it dissolves, take off heat and leave aside to cool down.

4. Add this to your food processor, mix with 4 ounces strawberries, cream cheese, lemon juice and stevia and blend well.
5. Add ½ cup heavy cream, stir well and spread this over crust.
6. Top with 8 ounces strawberries and 16 ounces heavy cream and keep in the fridge for 2 hours before slicing and serving.

Enjoy!

Nutrition: calories 234, fat 23, fiber 2, carbs 6, protein 7

Delicious Chocolate Pie

This special pie will impress your loved ones for sure!

Preparation time: 3 hours 10 minutes
Cooking time: 20 minutes
Servings: 10
Ingredients:

For the crust:
- ½ teaspoon baking powder
- 1 and ½ cup almond crust
- A pinch of salt
- 1/3 cup stevia
- 1 egg
- 1 and ½ teaspoons vanilla extract
- 3 tablespoons butter
- 1 teaspoon butter for the pan

For the filling:
- 1 tablespoon vanilla extract
- 4 tablespoons butter
- 4 tablespoons sour cream
- 16 ounces cream cheese
- ½ cup cut stevia
- ½ cup cocoa powder
- 2 teaspoons granulated stevia
- 1 cup whipping cream
- 1 teaspoon vanilla extract

Directions:
1. Grease a spring form pan with 1 teaspoon butter and leave aside for now.
2. In a bowl, mix baking powder with 1/3 cup stevia, a pinch of salt and almond flour and stir.
3. Add 3 tablespoons butter, egg and 1 and ½ teaspoon vanilla extract, stir until you obtain a dough.
4. Press this well into spring form pan, introduce in the oven at 375 degrees F and bake for 11 minutes.

5. Take pie crust out of the oven, cover with tin foil and bake for 8 minutes more.
6. Take it again out of the oven and leave it aside to cool down.
7. Meanwhile, in a bowl, mix cream cheese with 4 tablespoons butter, sour cream, 1 tablespoon vanilla extract, cocoa powder and ½ cup stevia and stir well.
8. In another bowl, mix whipping cream with 2 teaspoons stevia and 1 teaspoon vanilla extract and stir using your mixer.
9. Combine the 2 mixtures, pour into pie crust, spread well, introduce in the fridge for 3 hours and then serve.

Nutrition: calories 450, fat 43, fiber 3, carbs 7, protein 7

Tasty Cheesecakes

This is a keto friendly dessert idea you must try!

Preparation time: 10 minutes
Cooking time: 15 minutes
Servings: 9

Ingredients:
For the cheesecakes:
- 2 tablespoons butter
- 8 ounces cream cheese
- 3 tablespoons coffee
- 3 eggs
- 1/3 cup swerve
- 1 tablespoon caramel syrup, sugar free

For the frosting:
- 3 tablespoons caramel syrup, sugar free
- 3 tablespoons butter
- 8 ounces mascarpone cheese, soft
- 2 tablespoons swerve

Directions:
1. In your blender, mix cream cheese with eggs, 2 tablespoons butter, coffee, 1 tablespoon caramel syrup and 1/3 cup swerve and pulse very well.
2. Spoon this into a cupcakes pan, introduce in the oven at 350 degrees F and bake for 15 minutes.

3. Leave aside to cool down and then keep in the freezer for 3 hours.
4. Meanwhile, in a bowl, mix 3 tablespoons butter with 3 tablespoons caramel syrup, 2 tablespoons swerve and mascarpone cheese and blend well.
5. Spoon this over cheesecakes and serve them.

Enjoy!

Nutrition: calories 254, fat 23, fiber 0, carbs 1, protein 5

Raspberry And Coconut Dessert

They are easy to make and they taste delicious!

Preparation time: 10 minutes
Cooking time: 5 minutes
Servings: 12

Ingredients:
- ½ cup coconut butter
- ½ cup coconut oil
- ½ cup raspberries, dried
- ¼ cup swerve
- ½ cup coconut, shredded

Directions:
1. In your food processor, blend dried berries very well.
2. Heat up a pan with the butter over medium heat.
3. Add oil, coconut and swerve, stir and cook for 5 minutes.
4. Pour half of this into a lined baking pan and spread well.
5. Add raspberry powder and also spread.
6. Top with the rest of the butter mix, spread and keep in the fridge for a while.
7. Cut into pieces and serve.

Enjoy!

Nutrition: calories 234, fat 22, fiber 2, carbs 4, protein 2

Tasty Chocolate Cups

Everyone will adore these chocolate delights!

Preparation time: 30 minutes
Cooking time: 5 minutes
Servings: 20

Ingredients:
- ½ cup coconut butter
- ½ cup coconut oil
- 3 tablespoons swerve
- ½ cup coconut, shredded
- 1.5 ounce cocoa butter
- 1 ounces chocolate, unsweetened
- ¼ cup cocoa powder
- ¼ teaspoon vanilla extract
- ¼ cup swerve

Directions:
1. In a pan, mix coconut butter with coconut oil, stir and heat up over medium heat.
2. Add coconut and 3 tablespoons swerve, stir well, take off heat, scoop into a lined muffins pan and keep in the fridge for 30 minutes.
3. Meanwhile, in a bowl, mix cocoa butter with chocolate, vanilla extract and ¼ cup swerve and stir well.
4. Place this over a bowl filled with boiling water and stir until everything is smooth.
5. Spoon this over coconut cupcakes, keep in the fridge for 15 minutes more and then serve.

Enjoy!

Nutrition: calories 240, fat 23, fiber 4, carbs 5, protein 2

Simple And Delicious Mousse

This is just hypnotizing! It's great!

Preparation time: 10 minutes
Cooking time: 0 minutes
Servings: 12

Ingredients:
- 8 ounces mascarpone cheese
- ¾ teaspoon vanilla stevia
- 1 cup whipping cream
- ½ pint blueberries
- ½ pint strawberries

Directions:
1. In a bowl, mix whipping cream with stevia and mascarpone and blend well using your mixer.
2. Arrange a layer of blueberries and strawberries in 12 glasses, then a layer of cream and so on.
3. Serve this mousse cold!

Enjoy!

Nutrition: calories 143, fat 12, fiber 1, carbs 3, protein 2

Simple Peanut Butter Fudge

You only need a few ingredients to make this tasty keto dessert!

Preparation time: 2 hours and 10 minutes
Cooking time: 2 minutes
Servings: 12

Ingredients:
- 1 cup peanut butter, unsweetened
- ¼ cup almond milk
- 2 teaspoons vanilla stevia
- 1 cup coconut oil
- A pinch of salt

For the topping:
- 2 tablespoons swerve
- 2 tablespoons melted coconut oil
- ¼ cup cocoa powder

Directions:
1. In a heat proof bowl, mix peanut butter with 1 cup coconut oil, stir and heat up in your microwave until it melts.
2. Add a pinch of salt, almond milk and stevia, stir well everything and pour into a lined loaf pan.
3. Keep in the fridge for 2 hours and then slice it.
4. In a bowl, mix 2 tablespoons melted coconut with cocoa powder and swerve and stir very well.
5. Drizzle the sauce over your peanut butter fudge and serve. Enjoy!

Nutrition: calories 265, fat 23, fiber 2, carbs 4, protein 6

Lemon Mousse

This is so refreshing and delicious!

Preparation time: 10 minutes
Cooking time: 0 minutes
Servings: 5

Ingredients:
- 1 cup heavy cream
- A pinch of salt
- 1 teaspoon lemon stevia
- ¼ cup lemon juice
- 8 ounces mascarpone cheese

Directions:
1. In a bowl, mix heavy cream with mascarpone and lemon juice and stir using your mixer.
2. Add a pinch of salt and stevia and blend everything.
3. Divide into dessert glasses and keep in the fridge until you serve.

Enjoy!

Nutrition: calories 265, fat 27, fiber 0, carbs 2, protein 4

Vanilla Ice Cream

Try this keto ice cream on a summer day!

Preparation time: 3 hours and 10 minutes
Cooking time: 0 minutes
Servings: 6

Ingredients:

- 4 eggs, yolks and whites separated
- ¼ teaspoon cream of tartar
- ½ cup swerve
- 1 tablespoon vanilla extract
- 1 and ¼ cup heavy whipping cream

Directions:

1. In a bowl, mix egg whites with cream of tartar and swerve and stir using your mixer.
2. In another bowl, whisk cream with vanilla extract and blend very well.
3. Combine the 2 mixtures and stir gently.
4. In another bowl, whisk egg yolks very well and then add the two egg whites mix.
5. Stir gently, pour this into a container and keep in the freezer for 3 hours before serving your ice cream.

Enjoy!

Nutrition: calories 243, fat 22, fiber 0, carbs 2, protein 4

Cheesecake Squares

They look so good!

Preparation time: 10 minutes
Cooking time: 20 minutes
Servings: 9

Ingredients:
- 5 ounces coconut oil, melted
- ½ teaspoon baking powder
- 4 tablespoons swerve
- 1 teaspoon vanilla
- 4 ounces cream cheese
- 6 eggs
- ½ cup blueberries

Directions:
1. In a bowl, mix coconut oil with eggs, cream cheese, vanilla, swerve and baking powder and blend using an immersion blender.
2. Fold blueberries, pour everything into a square baking dish, introduce in the oven at 320 degrees F and bake for 20 minutes.
3. Leave you cake to cool down, slice into squares and serve.

Enjoy!

Nutrition: calories 220, fat 2, fiber 0.5, carbs 2, protein 4

Tasty Brownies

These flourless keto brownies are excellent!

Preparation time: 10 minutes
Cooking time: 20 minutes
Servings: 12

Ingredients:
- 6 ounces coconut oil, melted
- 6 eggs
- 3 ounces cocoa powder
- 2 teaspoons vanilla
- ½ teaspoon baking powder
- 4 ounces cream cheese
- 5 tablespoons swerve

Directions:
1. In a blender, mix eggs with coconut oil, cocoa powder, baking powder, vanilla, cream cheese and swerve and stir using a mixer.
2. Pour this into a lined baking dish, introduce in the oven at 350 degrees F and bake for 20 minutes.
3. Slice into rectangle pieces when their cold and serve.

Enjoy!

Nutrition: calories 178, fat 14, fiber 2, carbs 3, protein 5

Chocolate Pudding

This pudding is so tasty!

Preparation time: 50 minutes
Cooking time: 5 minutes
Servings: 2

Ingredients:
- 2 tablespoons water
- 1 tablespoon gelatin
- 2 tablespoons maple syrup
- ½ teaspoon stevia powder
- 2 tablespoons cocoa powder
- 1 cup coconut milk

Directions:
1. Heat up a pan with the coconut milk over medium heat, add stevia and cocoa powder and stir well.
2. In a bowl, mix gelatin with water, stir well and add to the pan.
3. Stir well, add maple syrup, whisk again, divide into ramekins and keep in the fridge for 45 minutes.
4. Serve cold.

Enjoy!

Nutrition: calories 140, fat 2, fiber 2, carbs 4, protein 4

Vanilla Parfaits
These will make you fell amazing!

Preparation time: 10 minutes
Cooking time: 0 minutes
Servings: 4

Ingredients:
- 14 ounces canned coconut milk
- 1 teaspoon vanilla extract
- 10 drops stevia
- 4 ounces berries
- 2 tablespoons walnuts, chopped

Directions:
1. In a bowl, mix coconut milk with stevia and vanilla extract and whisk using your mixer.
2. IN another bowl, mix berries with walnuts and stir.
3. Spoon half of vanilla coconut mix into 4 jars, add a layer of berries and top with the rest of the vanilla mix.
4. Top with berries and walnuts mix, introduce in the fridge until you serve it.

Enjoy!

Nutrition: calories 400, fat 23, fiber 4, carbs 6, protein 7

Simple Avocado Pudding

This is so easy to make at home and it follows keto principles!

Preparation time: 10 minutes
Cooking time: 0 minutes
Servings: 4

Ingredients:
- 2 avocados, pitted, peeled and chopped
- 2 teaspoons vanilla extract
- 80 drops stevia
- 1 tablespoon lime juice
- 14 ounces canned coconut milk

Directions:
1. In your blender, mix avocado with coconut milk, vanilla extract, stevia and lime juice, blend well, spoon into dessert bowls and keep in the fridge until you serve it.

Enjoy!

Nutrition: calories 150, fat 3, fiber 3, carbs 5, protein 6

Mint Delight

It has such a fresh texture and taste!

Preparation time: 2 hours and 10 minutes
Cooking time: 0 minutes
Servings: 3

Ingredients:
- ½ cup coconut oil, melted
- 3 stevia drops
- 1 tablespoon cocoa powder

For the pudding:
- 1 teaspoon peppermint oil
- 14 ounces canned coconut milk
- 1 avocado, pitted, peeled and chopped
- 10 drops stevia

Directions:
1. In a bowl, mix coconut oil with cocoa powder and 3 drops stevia, stir well, transfer to a lined container and keep in the fridge for 1 hour.
2. Chop this into small pieces and leave aside for now.
3. In your blender, mix coconut milk with avocado, 10 drops stevia and peppermint oil and pulse well.
4. Add chocolate chips, fold them gently, divide pudding into bowls and keep in the fridge for 1 more hour.

Enjoy!

Nutrition: calories 140, fat 3, fiber 2, carbs 3, protein 4

Amazing Coconut Pudding

You've got to love this keto pudding!

Preparation time: 10 minutes
Cooking time: 10 minutes
Servings: 4

Ingredients:
- 1 and 2/3 cups coconut milk
- 1 tablespoon gelatin
- 6 tablespoons swerve
- 3 egg yolks
- ½ teaspoon vanilla extract

Directions:
1. In a bowl, mix gelatin with 1 tablespoon coconut milk, stir well and leave aside for now.
2. Put the rest of the milk into a pan and heat up over medium heat.
3. Add swerve, stir and cook for 5 minutes.
4. In a bowl, mix egg yolks with the hot coconut milk and vanilla extract, stir well and return everything to the pan.
5. Cook for 4 minutes, add gelatin and stir well.
6. Divide this into 4 ramekins and keep your pudding in the fridge until you serve it.

Enjoy!

Nutrition: calories 140, fat 2, fiber 0, carbs 2, protein 2

Special Pudding

You must try this pudding as well!

Preparation time: 4 hours and 10 minutes
Cooking time: 3 minutes
Servings: 2

Ingredients:
- 4 teaspoons gelatin
- ¼ teaspoon liquid stevia
- 1 cup coconut milk
- A pinch of cardamom, ground
- ¼ teaspoon ginger, ground
- A pinch of nutmeg, ground

Directions:
1. In a bowl, mix ¼ cup milk with gelatin and stir well.
2. Put the rest of the coconut milk in a pot and heat up over medium heat.
3. Add gelatin mix, stir, take off heat, leave aside to cool down and then keep in the fridge for 4 hours.
4. Transfer this to a food processor, add stevia, cardamom, nutmeg and ginger and blend for a couple of minutes.
5. Divide into dessert cups and serve cold.

Enjoy!

Nutrition: calories 150, fat 1, fiber 0, carbs 2, protein 6

Chocolate Biscotti

This is an easy and very tasty keto dessert idea!

Preparation time: 10 minutes
Cooking time: 12 minutes
Servings: 8

Ingredients:
- 2 tablespoons chia seeds
- 2 cups almonds
- 1 egg
- ¼ cup coconut oil
- ¼ cup coconut, shredded
- 2 tablespoons stevia
- ¼ cup cocoa powder
- A pinch of salt
- 1 teaspoon baking soda

Directions:
1. In your food processor, mix chia seeds with almonds and blend well.
2. Add coconut, egg, coconut oil, cocoa powder, a pinch of salt, baking soda and stevia and blend well.
3. Shape 8 biscotti pieces out of this dough, place on a lined baking sheet, introduce in the oven at 350 degrees and bake for 12 minutes.
4. Serve them warm or cold.

Enjoy!

Nutrition: calories 200, fat 2, fiber 1, carbs 3, protein 4

Special Dessert

Have you tried making brownies in a skillet before?

Preparation time: 10 minutes
Cooking time: 30 minutes
Servings: 4

Ingredients:
- 1 egg
- 1/3 cup cocoa powder
- 1/3 cup erythritol
- 7 tablespoons ghee
- A pinch of salt
- ½ teaspoon vanilla extract
- ¼ cup almond flour
- ¼ cup walnuts
- ½ teaspoon baking powder
- 1 tablespoon peanut butter

Directions:
1. Heat up a pan with 6 tablespoons ghee and the erythritol over medium heat, stir and cook for 5 minutes.
2. Transfer this to a bowl, add salt, vanilla extract and cocoa powder and whisk well.
3. Add egg and stir well again.
4. Add baking powder, walnuts and almond flour, stir the whole thing really well and pour into a skillet.
5. In a bowl, mix 1 tablespoon ghee with peanut butter, heat up in your microwave for a few seconds and stir well.

6. Drizzle this over brownies mix in the skillet, introduce in the oven at 350 degrees F and bake for 30 minutes.
7. Leave brownies to cool down, cut and serve.

Enjoy!

Nutrition: calories 223, fat 32, fiber 1, carbs 3, protein 6

Tasty Scones

Serve this keto dessert with a cup of tea and enjoy!

Preparation time: 10 minutes
Cooking time: 10 minutes
Servings: 10

Ingredients:
- ½ cup coconut flour
- 1 cup blueberries
- 2 eggs
- ½ cup heavy cream
- ½ cup ghee
- ½ cup almond flour
- A pinch of salt
- 5 tablespoons stevia
- 2 teaspoons vanilla extract
- 2 teaspoons baking powder

Directions:
1. In a bowl, mix almond flour with coconut flour, salt, baking powder and blueberries and stir well.
2. In another bowl, mix heavy cream with ghee, vanilla extract, stevia and eggs and stir well.
3. Combine the 2 mixtures and stir until you obtain your dough.
4. Shape 10 triangles from this mix, place them on a lined baking sheet, introduce in the oven at 350 degrees F and bake for 10 minutes.
Serve them cold.

Enjoy!

Nutrition: calories 130, fat 2, fiber 2, carbs 4, protein 3

www.ingramcontent.com/pod-product-compliance
Lightning Source LLC
Chambersburg PA
CBHW071823080526
44589CB00012B/895